Workforce Planning: 90 Day Action Plan™

Handbook

**How to Implement Successful
Workforce Planning
Strategies, Tools and Techniques**

Jeffrey H. Gross

TopGrade Workforce Planning
Hudson, Ohio

Published by TopGrade Workforce Planning, Hudson, OH

First Edition 2009, Second Printing 2018

Printed and bound in the United States of America.

Library of Congress-in-Publication Data

Gross, Jeffrey H.
    Workforce Planning: 90 Day Action Plan Handbook: How to Implement Successful Workforce Planning Strategies, Tools and Techniques / Jeffrey H. Gross
    p. cm.
    Includes bibliographical references and index.

    ISBN 978 - 0-9822567-0-1 (Paperback)
    LCCN: 2008911725

    1. Organizational Behavior. 2. Leadership. 3. Human Resources Management. 4. Strategic Planning. I. Gross, Jeffrey H. II. Title

TopGrade Workforce Planning
Hudson, Ohio, USA
www.workforceplanning2020.com

Table of Contents

Part II

Creating the Road Map

Why workforce planning has become popular ◊ Competition and complexity ◊ The future requires a better plan

Questions to consider ◊ A comprehensive program is necessary ◊ Design challenges ◊ Caution- actions that could undermine your program ◊ Recommendations for your program ◊ Adaptations to existing programs ◊ Steps for your taskforce ◊ Checklist for your organization

Part III

Moving From Reaction to Prediction

Why this module is important ◊Define the future worker ◊ How you can use this in your company ◊ What other companies are doing ◊ Overview of the process ◊ Your ideal organization ◊ Steps for your taskforce ◊ Strategic segmentation ◊ Future organizational structure ◊ Checklist for your organization

9. Metrics...156

Reliable measures will make the difference ◊ What are you doing intentionally? ◊ What other companies are doing ◊ Four basic approaches ◊ Steps for your taskforce ◊ How you can use this in your company ◊ Plug in these findings ◊ Checklist for your organization

Part VI

Designing Your 90 Day Action Plan

10. Incremental Steps...172

Co-creation improves proper design

11. The First 30 Days...177

Keep the faith ◊ Process overview

12. The Next 30 Days...181

The seeds, roots, branches and fruit ◊ Process overview

13. The Last 30 Days...186

Unbundle the modules ◊ Process overview ◊ Don't stop here

14. Closing Arguments...190

The definition ◊ The research ◊ The evidence ◊ The program ◊ 30-60-90 day action plan

Acknowledgements

A simple thank you is not sufficient to express my gratitude and appreciation to Fran, my life partner. Her unending support, being my biggest fan, and unfaltering prayers sustained and inspired me to keep going. She loved and encouraged me when I needed it the most.

I do want to acknowledge Becky McFarland for her editing skills and professional insight. She is a friend and contributed greatly to the finished project. Thanks Becky.

Preface

Our company focuses on research. We want to know the why, how and why not. During the process of creating *"Workforce Planning: 90 Day Action Plan Handbook,"* we strongly felt there was a critical unmet need to place a practical set of workforce planning tools into the hands of leaders and executives on a global basis. We did, however, underestimate how timely and popular the program and research would be.

The pending retirement of 76 million baby boomers is widely documented. Every month or so headlines pronounce "Workforce Crisis," so it is no secret that the face of the workforce is changing.

"Strategic human capital management is a pervasive challenge facing the federal government. The widespread lack of attention to strategic human capital management in the past has created a fundamental weakness in the federal government's ability to perform its missions economically, efficiently, and effectively."[1]

Even with all the publicity, many leaders have missed the opportunity to anticipate these workforce changes and plan accordingly. That is until now.

Sound Research is Our Strength

Research is one of the hallmarks of our company. We dig into a topic and after we have a thorough understanding of the field we craft solutions for today's business leaders. For our workforce planning programs, we researched, benchmarked and surveyed those companies with workforce planning programs. The results will be important to you. For example, according to a global survey we conducted in 2008, business leaders agree that workforce planning is a tool they can use to strategically impact their organizations.[2]

In addition, our research uncovered the illuminating insight; over 80% of surveyed Human Resource leaders recognize that they have to become more strategic to help their companies be more competitive. So that causes one to ask the question;

"What are you doing to become a more strategically important to your organization?"

We have found that it is very important in the field of workforce planning for you to network and learn from other companies. We have taken the time to do this for you. Throughout the **Handbook** we share our findings to help you understand what other companies are doing in their workforce planning programs so you can leverage these insights to save time and resources in implementing your program. You will find we have captured what companies are doing, what is effective and what needs improving.

If you are like the majority of business leaders throughout the globe, workforce planning is a hot topic and present on your mind. You also may have firsthand experience in the dynamics of change in the available labor and skills. One way you can counteract these affects is by bringing a formal workforce planning program to your company. When you do you can look forward to these benefits:

➤ Bringing a strategic outlook to the human capital equations.
➤ Enabling your organization to manage human capital more efficiently.

> ➢ Providing a deeper insight to the business needs for competencies.
> ➢ Addressing the long-term need for leadership in the future.
> ➢ Bringing HR to the table when it comes to becoming a more strategic partner to the line businesses.

In our view, many times workforce planning is misunderstood, undefined and seemingly too vast to relate to. It is popular to discuss but not widely accepted as necessary. This *Handbook* was written to drive value for your workforce planning program, value that will get to the core of your organization's human capital needs. We emphasize the need for holistic and systematic approaches which make intuitive and scientific sense.

> ➢ Do you currently think about your organization's systems and overall structure before recruiting talent?
> ➢ Do you truly understand what it takes to get work done, what competencies are needed and how they relate to your bench strength?
> ➢ Is the strategic business need at the forefront of all human capital decision making?
> ➢ Have you validated the HR delivery mechanisms you use to fulfill the human capital needs?

Workforce Planning New Strategic Tool

Workforce planning is a relatively new attempt to bring a quantitative view to HR. The literature in the field of workforce planning indicates that the early implementers were primarily governmental agencies. Many companies in the private sector have begun to take a strategic approach to their human capital planning as they seek to become more competitive.

In their research, *The Conference Board* determined that the majority of companies are *in-process* and not fully matured when it comes to implementing a strategic workforce plan. The researchers asked individuals from targeted companies how proficient they were in implementing and sustaining a workforce planning program. The responses for the most part were, "We're just getting started," or "We're not there yet."[3]

In our research we found nearly 85% of companies we evaluated had been *sustaining* a workforce planning program for fewer than five years. So take heart if this is a new area for you and your organization.

In the next decade, we predict workforce planning will become an essential building block of the HR toolkit. This **Handbook** *is intended to help make that vision a reality. Enjoy!*

Workforce Planning: 90 Day Action Plan™

Handbook

Introduction

Let's start with a strong dose of reality. Regardless the nature of your business, the changing demographics of the employee landscape are going to significantly impact your ability to recruit, train and promote the right person at the right time to keep your organization competitive. The evidence tells us that there will be fewer qualified and skilled professionals available in the workforce and it follows that the competition for the best talent will intensify. These are not speculative judgments; they are a reflection of what the future holds for all companies when it comes to strategic human capital decisions. Is it possible to predict that your company will escape the impact of these trends? The answer to that question is, *not very likely*. If you could predict and calculate the impact that these changes in the global workforce will have on your organization then you wouldn't need a strategic plan.

Take action and set the cornerstones of a strategic plan. When you do, you will be staking out a position in an uncertain world. Your proactive planning will send a message to your competition and customers that you intend to be a strategically designed, purpose-driven enterprise despite the consequences brought on by external forces.

In the process of guiding you through the **Handbook**, we start with digging into answers to the following questions. This is only a start; however, the real value comes after you have implemented a successful program, one which will work for your organization. We know you have questions about workforce planning programs. Our goal is to provide the answers to take you to the next level.

1. *Why this approach is unique.*

2. *What other companies are doing.*

3. *What are the actions that could undermine your program?*

4. *How you can use this in your company.*

> ## Why this approach is unique.

In our research we found workforce planning programs to be lacking a comprehensive approach. To fill this void we designed a process that is all-inclusive and encourages you to use it as an ongoing methodology to advance to a higher level of strategic business planning.

The differences in our program stand out immediately to the trained eye. Traditionally the three aspects of workforce planning include the future (or demand), the present (or supply) and the gap analysis leading to talent acquisition or training.

We start with a comprehensive set of modules as seen in figure p-1 showing the interconnected aspects of our process. Our program adds in separate, although equal, emphasis on modules for competencies and metrics. In our research we found these two areas were discussed but often missing in most programs and workforce planning processes. The more we investigated these modules the more we became convinced that they had to be a part of any process in order for it to be successful.

FIGURE P-1

Five Program Modules

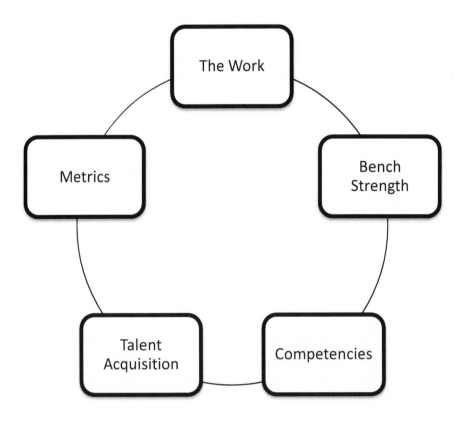

In the **Handbook** we introduce each module. Then we refine the definition and sharpen the focus on how it fits in the program. Next, we guide you through the techniques which will help you identify high-value implementation targets, and begin to structure a program for your organization that accommodates *the work* and *worker* of the future.

➤ What other companies are doing.

In each section of the **Handbook** we put emphasis on the research we have conducted and share with you the insights on what other companies are doing in workforce planning. This icon, signifying a "snapshot in time," will indicate the research findings which make our program stand out from the others.

When it comes to being competitive and impacting your organization's success, our belief is that your workforce or human capital is nearly always described as the "difference maker." Have you considered the following questions?

- ✓ Are we as competitive as we need to be?
- ✓ Does our human capital stack up against our competition?
- ✓ If our company was a sports team would we be at the top of our division?
- ✓ Do I know who the best leaders are in your industry?
- ✓ How would our best leaders stack up with the others in our industry?
- ✓ Do we really do strategic work in HR?
- ✓ When was the last time I did something for our organization that was considered a "difference maker?"

There is no substitute for making intelligent and informed decisions. Every day business leaders make dozens of choices which impact the future of their operations. For instance, when a large scale operation chooses to improve the logistics or supply chain function they may decide to bring in experts and invest in a technology such as SAP or some other enterprise resource planning system. Before these savvy business executives commit the capital to such a solution, they use a thought-out progression of steps. They are seeking to understand the need, investigate the options, study the market intelligence and engineer a methodology to guide their decision process.

As thoughtful and careful as these executives appear to be when it comes to making an operating decision they are routinely lax when it comes to making decisions for their human capital needs. Even with the best of intentions, business leaders regularly make poor, uninformed and expedient selection or hiring decisions. We feel it often is not their fault because the same vigorous methodology used in operating decisions is not used when making decisions that affect the workforce.

What often is lost is the clarity of visualizing the impact a poor decision can have when the wrong person is selected for hiring or promotion. Most organizations have horror stories of making a bad hiring decision and can recall with 20/20 hindsight how they suffered the consequences. If this happens repeatedly and you make a series of bad decisions then the disastrous long-term effects will haunt your organization.[1]

We realize that mistakes occur because you can't always make an accurate prediction matching a person and position. We are suggesting that reducing the poor decisions may be easier than you think and the impact far more positive and cost effective.

Planning for any outcome in business is necessary yet HR leaders too often seem to be in a reactive mode. They face the constant challenge of seeking to understand the impact many different trends have on their organization. Workforce planning comes in many different forms but is not often addressed as a comprehensive approach.

By taking a proactive approach and instituting a comprehensive and strategic human capital response in the short term, the cost and risk will be minimized. In the long term, the impact will give your organization a competitive edge over your competition and a strategic program for the human capital, your "difference maker."

> ## ➢ **Caution - actions that could undermine your program.**

In our research we have not only identified areas for you to benchmark and use in your program we also have identified *cautions* which would undermine the success of your implementation. This icon represents those areas we feel you should be on alert for as they could slow or derail your process and impact the potential for success.

By alerting you to the areas which could cause your organization a setback, we are helping you to face the hard facts of organizational change. We introduce you to actual scenarios and challenges we know you will face. Then we describe the results from our research on benchmarked companies. Lastly, we offer solutions in advance of you having to experience these disappointments.

In the majority of cases, the lack of understanding about the systemic structure, or interrelationships, that exist in a workforce planning model culminates in failed attempts to implement a program. We want to prevent that from happening to you. By taking a holistic view and following the programmatic approach we have designed you will reduce the risk of failure and improve the opportunities for dramatic success.

> ### How you can use this in your company.

You may be wondering what you need to do to get started. We would like to challenge your thinking about workforce planning. To help you transform your operations, we have identified traditional HR delivery protocols that companies have changed or adapted based on what they learned from their workforce planning process. We have studied researched and surveyed organizations that have implemented and sustained workforce planning programs.

Your tool set is all inclusive. The forms we have designed and the techniques recommended for implementing your program complement each other and fit together like pieces of a puzzle.

The different techniques include worksheets and guided learning questions for your taskforce members. Their responses will bring together the necessary information to guide you through staged success points to implement each module.

In case you need additional help, you may find our workshops valuable. As you advance to a higher level of effectiveness in your workforce planning you may find a need for additional coaching, please reach out and we would be glad to help.

What is In This Handbook?

The **Handbook** was written for use in all aspects of implementing a workforce planning program. It is intended for any individual in a leadership role who has a desire to learn and is focused on making his/her organization more effective. The materials and procedures outlined are based on extensive research and benchmarking. Our "how-to" approach provides both theory and fundamentals to implement a successful program in a concise and easy-to-use formula.

We have developed a guided learning process and crafted the steps necessary for you to take and implement the core modules of workforce planning while adapting them to your organizational needs.

As we benchmarked the crucial aspects of workforce planning we were able to synthesize the aspects you will need including:

➢ Key techniques used when implementing a program.
➢ Challenges companies face when implementing a program.
➢ Changes companies have made in their current programs after implementing workforce planning.
➢ Areas companies expect to improve as a result of executing a workforce planning program.
➢ Workforce planning fundamentals you can implement in a modular format.
➢ Specific techniques you can use to overcome objections and gain buy-in.

In each section we provide a framework for you to take and build your own program. We start by giving you the steps to begin setting objectives. Then we lead you to begin to visualize the organizational structure of your company, and define the specific areas to customize for your program.

Lastly, by using our customized forms and tools we direct you on the path to crafting a more competitive organization, one which will be flexible and adaptable to ride the wave of change.

Who Can Benefit From This Handbook?

This book is a tremendous resource for learning about the specifics necessary to instill a workforce planning program, and to answer the question, "Who will benefit from this *Handbook*?"

Individuals Leaders

➢ HR leaders realizing they have a need to become more strategic when it comes to understanding their human capital needs in order to become more competitive.
➢ HR leaders or business leaders seeking to understand fundamentals and essentials for workforce planning.
➢ Any executive desiring to make an impact through better human capital planning.
➢ Any individual that has a leadership role and is responsible to hire, train, develop and promote others.

Teams and Taskforce Members

➢ Any team or group of individuals responsible for implementing or sustaining a workforce planning program.

Organizations

➢ Companies seeking to improve their ability to match their human capital with their business needs.

➢ Among other benefits, it will make your company more efficient in the following ways:

o   The cost-to-hire ratios will drop.

o   The need to go outside a company to hire
    will be dictated by the business strategy, not
    by the head count.

o   The ability to retain, train, and develop
    leaders will improve because the training
    outcome will be predicted in advance of the
    curriculum design.

This program undoubtedly will give your HR group a chance to define and implement a program that will drive for results and encourage you to partner more effectively in any strategic realignment. Whether your company is faced with instituting a course correction, is going through a merger, or chooses to bring in new product lines of business, they all require you to evaluate and consider the human side necessary to bring about the successful changes. Workforce planning will be the tool of choice.

How to Use This Handbook

We designed the *Handbook* to be used as a reference guide and implementation resource. These icons indicate special sections and forms for your guided learning.

What other companies are doing. These recommendations and insights are based on our own research.

How you can use this in your company.
These sections are highlighted to draw specific
examples for you to use in your own organization.

***Caution – actions that could undermine
your program.*** In our ***Handbook*** we
periodically identify areas that other companies
have alerted us to as possible barriers to your
implementation.

Steps for your taskforce. Throughout the
Handbook we have designed forms, worksheets,
questionnaires and thought-starters intended to
guide your thinking and processes so you can
customize the material for your organization.

Tools designed for this program. These
forms are found in-depth in the appendix as well
as we highlight them throughout the ***Handbook.***

90 Day Action Plan. We have designed this
program in 30 day increments and selected specific
areas and tools for your organizational needs.
Look for this icon to relate to specific goals for your
plan.

Just like a detailed road map guides you through rough geographical terrain, this **Handbook** will steer you through the mountains and valleys of implementing a successful workforce planning program.

A recent survey conducted by the international consulting firm McKinsey&Company states "only HR can translate a business strategy into a talent pipeline strategy." It is time, the author further points out, for workforce planning to become a strategic component of a business plan.[2]

This program and materials give you a methodology and tool-set to begin the implementation of a customizable workforce planning program. The pages that follow provide the steps and necessary methods to take. Use any module you see as a fit, or implement the entire program.

Our mission is to bring not only the research, insights and strategic components to the mass market, but also to offer the practical tools for implementing a successful program for any size company. You will find that our process is easily customizable and evidence-based, and will be effective in your organization.

That is our commitment to you.

Plans are essential management tools. In this section you learn what it takes to start a dialogue based on a research-driven protocol.

Part I

Making
The
Business Case

1. Workforce Planning: Why Now?

In an effort to become more competitive, companies have "right-sized" their employee populations and often looked to talent acquisition technology (i.e. posting open positions on the internet and applicant tracking systems) to make higher quality hires. We found these solutions over promise and under deliver resulting in the need for new answers to the same problems. Rarely have companies made a conscious decision to approach their human capital the way they do their fiscal or real estate capital.

What will make a workforce planning program a fit for your organization? When you decide to set in motion a workforce planning program the specific reason and tipping point may not be clear. It will be dependent on several issues you face as an organization. You may be experiencing serious human capital challenges in succession planning, recruiting or possibly experienced layoffs recently. You may be curious about the workforce planning process. In any case, you have selected the right reference tool to advance your knowledge in this field and we thank you.

When we research companies, we always ask, "What made you decide *now is the time* to put a workforce planning program in place?" In these following pages we share many of the answers companies gave us.

In one project we asked HR professionals how satisfied they were with their ability to match up the human capital capabilities with the business unit needs. This was regardless if they had a workforce planning program or not. We used the following scale to separate their responses. Each respondent was required to select one of the following answers. [1]

- ❖ ***Unsatisfied*** – Do very little planning for our human capital needs and mostly are reactive to the business needs.

- ❖ ***Somewhat Satisfied*** – We try to plan for and execute on the human capital needs but still fall short more often than not.

- ❖ ***Satisfied*** – We do plan for our human capital needs and fulfill the business needs about one-half of the time.

- ❖ ***Very Satisfied*** – We are good at planning and most of the time we are ahead of the curve for matching the human capital needs of the business units.

- ❖ ***Highly Satisfied*** – We are excellent at planning for the human capital needs and follow-through with low-cost and high quality talent for our strategic business needs.

The answers they gave were enlightening and may surprise you. As you can see in this chart, the results show that **over 70%** of the participants reported they were satisfied with their ability to meet their strategic human capital needs *less than half* of the time.

FIGURE 1-1

Scale for Survey

Unsatisfied – 3.2%

Somewhat Satisfied – 35.5%

Satisfied – 32.3%

Very Satisfied – 19.4%

Highly Satisfied – 3.2%

Unsure – 6.5%

Being able to meet the human capital needs required to execute their business strategy only 50% of the time is a candid response from these HR executives. It also reflects how poorly companies plan and deliver the most important resource a company has, their human resource.

If you are asked, "How satisfied are you with your ability to meet the strategic human capital needs of your business?" What would be your answer?

_____

_____

_____

_____

_____

_____

_____

_____

Our Research Brings Focus

Our organization conducted an international webcast on workforce planning in February 2008, 509 individuals registered representing 33 different countries. We conducted a pulse-poll and asked how many of the participants were actively engaged in a workforce planning program. We found that 68% of the participants had no workforce planning strategy what so ever. [2]

In one of our recent benchmarking studies, the respondent's represented 15 industry sectors and all had global business operations. Over 50% of the participating companies had over 5,000 employees. The titles of the individuals surveyed included Manager, Director, Vice President and Senior/Executive Vice President. Over 90% of the respondents were HR leaders in their respective organizations. The following list is a representation of the industry groups surveyed.

- Aerospace
- Biotech
- Consumer Products
- Energy
- Financial Services
- Food Distribution
- Forestry/Fishing/Mining
- Government
- Healthcare
- IT/Telecom
- Legal
- Manufacturing
- Retail/Wholesale
- Services
- Transportation

As diverse as this group was, they responded in similar fashion (figure 1-2) when asked the proverbial question "Why would you do a workforce planning program?" HR leaders told us that, for the future, *workforce planning* is the tool of choice for improving their ability to match the human capital capabilities with the business unit needs. To make a strong argument for implementing a workforce planning process, leverage our research results on companies that have implemented a program.

Even though the media headlines emphasize the retiring baby-boomers as a need to consider workforce planning, nine out of ten companies in our research felt the reason for workforce planning was to incorporate a *strategic solution* for their human capital planning. [3]

FIGURE 1-2

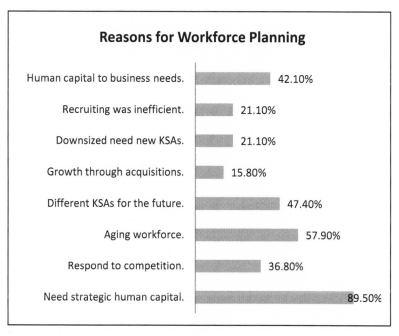

KSAs (Knowledge, Skills, Attributes)

What are your reasons for implementing workforce planning?

How do your reasons stack-up against the companies in our research?

How will you answer the questions when your leaders ask, "What are you doing to align the human capital with their business needs?"

Incorporate these responses into your 90 Day Action Plan.

_____

_____

_____

_____

_____

_____

_____

_____

_____

2. Global Workforce Trends

The argument for a workforce planning program is found in these undeniable truths.

❖ *The worker is changing.*

❖ *The work is changing.*

❖ *The skills and competencies you need to compete are changing.*

❖ *The competition for the workers possessing those competencies and skills is intensifying as the labor market changes.*

As far back as 1997 a study for the U.S. Department of Labor, Employment and Training Administration found that the dramatic decline in the available workforce population would impact the overall labor market. They found that the population that is 55 and older will increase more sharply between 1995 and 2025 than any other age group. The dominance of the baby boomers on the labor market will continue until 2025 when the surviving part of that generation will have exceeded 60 years of age. Overall, the Census Bureau projects that the aging trend in the nation will be affected by the baby boom generation until 2040. [1]

What the labor pool will look like...

✓ The overall rate of U.S. workforce growth was 30% in the 1970s, 12% in the 1990s to present, but it is anticipated to level off at 2 to 3% in 2010 and beyond.

✓ By 2010, the number of 35 to 44 year olds, those normally expected to move into senior management ranks, will not grow but will decline by 10%.

✓ By 2010, the number of U.S. workers ages 45 to 54 will grow by 21%; the number of 55 to 64 year olds will grow by 52%.

✓ In Europe, the pool of workers ages 35 to 44 is expected to shrink by 19% in the United Kingdom, 27% in Germany, and 9% in Italy.

✓ In Japan, workers ages 35 to 44 will shrink by 10%, and in China, by 8%. [2]

There is no doubt the labor pool is shrinking but not just shrinking as a result of retirements. It is far more complicated and it is a cause for concern. For example, the changes we have witnessed in entire industry sectors present new dilemmas for workforce planning programs.
One of the obvious wide-reaching impacts the world felt was the decline of the automotive industry at the end of

2008. The rise in unemployment, drop in capital spending and intense competition of the market place left many leaders scratching their heads as they attempted to fabricate an answer to their workforce needs in the coming years. These changes only validate the need for an overhaul of how companies plan and execute their human capital needs both short and long term.

The speed at which these changes seem to overtake the world's largest corporations is mind boggling. There is no time to back into a plan. Workforce planning needs to be at the front of the strategic plan.

In addition to the predictable shortfall in labor and skills, managers seem perplexed as aging workers who possess critical knowledge are replaced by not only a younger group, but one which will be put in charge with little time to prepare.

Trends are Important Indicators

As recognized by William Rothwell in *Beyond Training and Development,* 1996, four trends have impacted workforce planning include: [3]

1. Keeping pace with rapid external environmental change.

2. Establishing high-performance work environments.

3. Organizing work activities in innovative ways.

4. Upgrading employee competencies in real time.

With the first trend, phrases like *globalization, sustainability, downsizing, right-sizing, market share,* all bring images of how some external element seems to determine what action to take. In *Thriving on Chaos,* 1988, Tom Peter's states, "there is no prescription which says it outright, yet it lurks on every page. It is the revolution to which the title refers. The world has turned up-side down and it appears to be turning every which way at an accelerating pace." [4]

The second trend describes how efforts by many companies are focused on high-performance work environments. These environments are intended to have more flexibility on organizational structure allowing for more prompt decision making and fewer layers of command. Interestingly, a U.S. Department of Labor multiyear study found that when companies decided to move toward a high-performance workplace they often found that their workers lacked the right competencies to bring about the needed changes. This insight reflects the rationale for our including competency modeling in our program.

The third trend identified is one where the work activities are organized in increasingly innovative ways. The intention being that these changes would give the worker more control over the work he/she did from start to finish. This trend includes an effort at re-engineering the work so there are fewer steps, more cross function sharing and resulting in productivity improvements.

The fourth and final trend identified by Rothwell is how employees themselves are finding that they must prepare to continually upgrade their competencies in real time. The emphasis for understanding the competencies and skills needed then is placed squarely on the shoulders of the employee. [5]

These four trends identified by Rothwell link seamlessly with the indicators showing the labor pool changes. There are more trends to watch. Our benchmark research indicates the global trends in the coming chapters.

State Government

In 2000, over 50% of the individuals employed by the State of Washington were age 45 or older. The future needs of the government programs and infrastructure would be dramatically impacted as turnover would increase dramatically as a result of retirements.

> *"As the problems facing society and state government become more complex, and risks associated with solving them grow, the importance of attracting and retaining state employees with necessary skills and commitment increases."*

> *"Achieving results in government, probably more than any other business, is highly dependent upon the quality, judgment, and motivation of its workforce. Maintaining that workforce today requires careful management planning to be an attractive competitive employer."* [6]

Global Strategic Challenges

According to a 2007 study in the *McKinsey Quarterly*, many companies are "ill prepared to change" even though they are faced with massive social and economic trends which will require organizational change. This study emphasizes the evidence executives *know they must change* to become more competitive, yet they resist the notion it is *they* who need to change. We see a parallel with this hesitancy to implement change. Companies claim they understand the benefits of workforce planning but are slow to make the changes necessary. The study results included the following insights: [7]

✓ 47% of companies don't have the right people in place to lead the changes.

✓ 72% of executives in the study say the needed new people will come from external sources.

✓ In addition, when the people come from internal promotions 79% of respondents say they are not up to the skills needed to face the changes they will be going through.

Our Research Brings Focus

We asked HR leaders to indicate the global workforce trends that will impact their organizations. Then we asked them to tell us how prepared they are to do something about these trends. They responded with insights about their organizations that undoubtedly will help other companies as they seek to gain a competitive foothold in their industry sector.

The participants were asked to evaluate the following global workforce trends as having an impact on their business and to indicate one of three responses: *No Impact, Some Impact,* or *Very Much Impact.* [8]

The trends they rated are:

- ➤ *Tightening Labor Market*
- ➤ *Industry Consolidations*
- ➤ *Availability of Technology*
- ➤ *Competition for Technical/Managerial Talent*
- ➤ *Emerging Markets*
- ➤ *Larger and More Complex Organizations*
- ➤ *Competition for Talent Will Intensify*
- ➤ *Shifting Organizational Structures*
- ➤ *Aging Population in the Labor Market*
- ➤ *Retirement of Workers*
- ➤ *Availability of Skilled Workers*
- ➤ *Global Talent Challenges*

After the respondents determined the degree of impact these trends would have on their organizations over the next five years, we asked them to determine how prepared they were for meeting these challenges. The scoring for this area included: *Not Very Prepared, Somewhat Prepared*, or *Very Prepared*.

Once we had their responses and began to evaluate the answers (figure 2-1) we compared the two sets of responses. We were able to contrast these answers and we charted the two extreme ends of the questionnaire. In order to create the appropriate impact and understanding, we contrast the scores of being prepared and understanding impact. This chart titled *Global Strategic Challenges* contrasts *Very Prepared* and *Very Much Impact* (the two extremes of the scoring dimension). Clearly there are significant gaps.

FIGURE 2-1

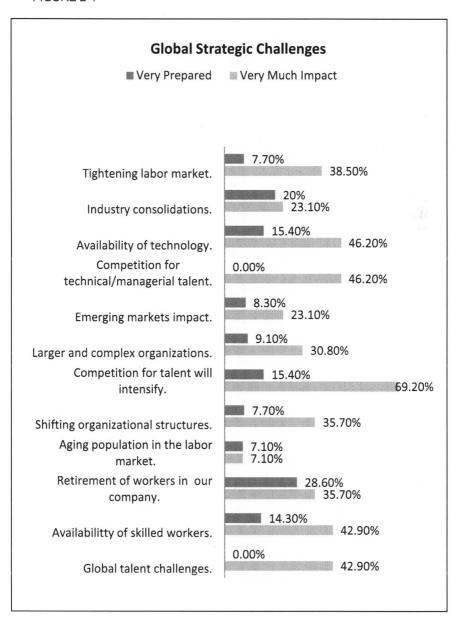

Global Strategic Challenges

■ Very Prepared　　■ Very Much Impact

Tightening labor market.
- 7.70%
- 38.50%

Industry consolidations.
- 20%
- 23.10%

Availability of technology.
- 15.40%
- 46.20%

Competition for technical/managerial talent.
- 0.00%
- 46.20%

Emerging markets impact.
- 8.30%
- 23.10%

Larger and complex organizations.
- 9.10%
- 30.80%

Competition for talent will intensify.
- 15.40%
- 69.20%

Shifting organizational structures.
- 7.70%
- 35.70%

Aging population in the labor market.
- 7.10%
- 7.10%

Retirement of workers in our company.
- 28.60%
- 35.70%

Availabilitty of skilled workers.
- 14.30%
- 42.90%

Global talent challenges.
- 0.00%
- 42.90%

Based on our findings, we can share the following results implying the respondents recognize the impact that global workforce trends will have on their ability to compete. [9]

Their responses can be summarized in these high level insights:

A. *The competition for talent will intensify and securing the best talent will be more challenging. There is agreement that there will be shortages of skills and a shrinking access to skilled workers needed caused by tightening of labor markets.*

B. *Complicating the competitive market place for talent will be a test to find and acquire the competencies these companies are seeking to compensate for the gaps in skills brought on by an aging workforce.*

C. *In a larger context, organizational structures will need to <u>adapt and implement</u> more flexibility to meet the challenges brought on by emerging markets.*

D. *In some sectors these organizational structures will be impacted by industry consolidations through mergers or acquisitions, creating a new playing field.*

All of these trends emphasize the components of a workforce planning initiative.

Questions to ponder:

1. Do we consider trends?
2. How do we incorporate them into our
   workforce planning?
3. Are we followers or leaders in our business
   segments?
4. Where can we improve when it comes to
   considering trends?
5. Do we research a program before we
   implement it?
6. How much data do we use before deciding to
   select a process?

*Incorporate these responses into your *90 Day*
Action Plan.*

_____

_____

_____

_____

_____

_____

_____

Checklist for your organization

In our opinion, it is not sufficient to know you are facing change; you must act to confront it. This checklist is for you to begin to consider how your organization is prepared to face this series of trends and challenges.

It has been crafted to give you enough ammunition to begin to build a business case for workforce planning for your organization. In case there is still not enough information or material in the *Handbook* please contact us. Possibly a customized assessment will be a tool you will find useful. In the mean time, work your way through the rest of the book and customizable exercises.

Also, it may help to have several team members or a taskforce read the book and begin to do these exercises in concert with others on the team. Once you have an organized effort and you can compare responses and the prospective to implement a successful program will improve.

FIGURE 2-2

Checklist of Global Trends

Global Trends	Impact on Your Organization?	How Prepared?
Tightening Labor Market		
Industry Consolidations		
Availability of Technology		
Competition for Technical/Managerial Talent		
Impact of Emerging Markets		
Larger and More Complex Organizations		
Competition for Talent Will Intensify		
Shifting Organizational Structures		
Aging Population in the Labor Market		
Retirement of Workers in Our Company		
Availability of Skilled Workers		
Global Talent Challenges		
Tightening Labor Market		

We are now going to decode workforce planning so you will have the insights to craft your own program.

Part II

Creating the Road Map

3. Strategic Workforce Planning Defined

Workforce planning is a comprehensive and strategic tool which will make your organization more competitive.

In many sources of literature and research, the discussions on strategic workforce planning take various shapes. In a study by The Conference Board titled *Strategic Workforce Planning* the authors define it as "the analytic, forecasting, and planning process that connects and directs talent management activities to ensure an organization has the right people in the right places at the right time and at the right price to execute its business strategy." [1]

Strategic workforce planning is the alignment of human capital with the diagnosed business needs. It is a comprehensive approach to delivering HR processes, and when properly executed, each business entity will have the right person in the right job at the right time. Workforce planning programs have to deliver on these points.

Workforce Planning Incorporates...

- ❖ The skills and competencies which relate to the defined work as understood in present reality and future need.

- ❖ The designated needs are contrasted against an existing inventory revealing gaps.

- ❖ These gaps are subsequently planned to be addressed through external acquisition, professional development, or succession planning.

- ❖ The success of the program is determined by the same standard of excellence by which any business venture is measured.

- ❖ It has to make the company more profitable.

Workforce Planning has Gained Popularity

When it comes to responding to "why" workforce planning is needed, officials in the state of Washington emphasized the benefits to the agency leadership. They described that a properly implemented and utilized workforce planning program allows a manager to have the strategic basis for making human capital decisions. It allows them to anticipate change rather than being surprised by events.

The overall success for a state agency or a private company depends on having the employees with the right competencies in the right job and at the right time. It is through a workforce planning formula and comprehensive approach that these tools are placed in the hands of the line managers. Without this process they are flying blind and executing from instinct; or worse, from only looking at the past set of experiences. Workforce planning brings the three aspects of demand for the future, supply of the present, and gaps of competency needs in a quantifiable way. [2]

Competition and Complexity

Companies who compete in global markets have to move faster to stay ahead of their competition and that means they need "knowledge workers" more than any other category of worker. The nature of the current global economy and market place has proportionally advanced the degree of complexity with which each organization operates. Yet, most companies use an organizational structure designed for the 20th century and it inhibits them from being able to tap the mind power and talents of the workers they have.

In the 1900s, following the industrial revolution, the need was for high numbers of physical bodies to run assembly lines and move materials. In the 2000s the "knowledge worker" is a valued commodity that exemplifies the *future-state* of the workforce. This individual defines the workforce of the next decade. He/she has more education, is technically savvy and makes the workforce more demographically diverse than any time in history.

Corporate America in 2000 and beyond will depend on its employees to make decisions and solve problems not to provide manual labor. The need is mind power, not back power, and that is where the competitive advantage is. Because of changes in technology, companies have the ability to get products out of R&D to the end user faster than ever before. These changes reflect the utilization of mental power and knowledge necessary to navigate the labyrinth of the market place. For the future, the need will be to free up these individuals and not stifle them with a poorly functioning organizational structure. [3]

The Future Requires a Better Plan

To respond to the need for the new workforce, let's begin by mentally advancing into the future. Imagine that the old corporate culture, the one we live in today, with maximizing short-term return on investment (ROI) and the tendency to reinvent the wheel at every whim is gone.

The organization of the future will have a new strategic human capital structure. The business units will be able to focus on expanding world markets, meet the rising customer demand, employ knowledge workers who are the value of the company and focus on renewable and sustainable business models. Workforce planning is the only way to compete and win.

In our view, workforce planning is not simply a new fix-it for human capital challenges. It needs to be measured and adapted against performance goals and metrics which follow the business needs. It also needs to be sustainable and not have a draining or detrimental impact on the fiscal health of the company. Also, the workforce planning program you choose to implement needs to be seen as an asset and not a liability.

We believe as the authors of *Mobilizing Minds*, Lowell Bryan and Claudia Joyce do, that now is the time for the leaders of organizations to begin to take the stance that human capital can be leveraged as a strategic imperative and seen as a "high-return, low-risk opportunity for investment." [4]

4. Program Design

> *"At this, the dawning of the 21st
> century, it is not surprising that the top
> leadership teams in large companies
> are having trouble finding their way to
> a new organizational model that fits
> the needs of the modern, digital, global
> economy. Nor is it surprising that the
> frontline workers and midlevel
> managers are finding their work a
> hard struggle."* [1]

During the first 30 days of your workforce planning program it will be necessary to incorporate the principles which will sustain your organization through the program. In this chapter we guide you to design a program that will be your road map to the future. We discussed the definition of workforce planning and now you can begin to structure the fundamentals. We start by *asking questions* and recommending your taskforce dig into the organization for the answers.

The right questions will lead your organization through a series of principles culminating in an applied answer. The fundamentals of workforce planning have to be about the *application* and not just discussion and planning.

Our research shows that when companies were in the formative stages of considering workforce planning, they stated that they clearly had a need to become more strategic when trying to understand the human capital needs of the company. The steps these companies took to consider workforce planning included digging into how effective they were and how strategically they filled the needs for talent through acquiring or developing specific competencies. [2]

At this point you should have selected a taskforce to spearhead the workforce planning strategy and program needs. As the individuals in the taskforce take on their responsibilities you will need to have a series of meetings to outline the "rules of engagement" and set clear goals and timelines. Crafting a selected group of "brainstorming" items and agenda bullet points will help you get off on the right step. Below are suggestions for guiding these initial sessions.

Questions to consider:

- ✓ Do I consider my organization prepared to implement a workforce planning program?

- ✓ How well positioned is the organization to respond to effects of future trends?

- ✓ What action steps can the organization take to meet the threats and opportunities posed by future trends?

- ✓ How can the organization maximize its strengths and minimize its weaknesses as the future unfolds in the present?

✓ What are the changes you need for the organization in structure and alignment?

✓ Who are the leaders in these key areas to partner with?

In addition to the business unit leaders and designated taskforce individuals you should have recruited an executive from the senior leadership to be part of the team.

A Comprehensive Program Is Necessary

For a workforce planning program to succeed, it is critical for you to implement a comprehensive approach. In this next section we discuss the design and implementation steps you will need as well as share significant insights and best practices from our research.

Workforce planning should be approached as a process. You will need to gather the necessary research and decision tools needed to execute a successful methodology. This area is intended to cover the essentials you will need and provide the confidence in your process design. Our benchmarking studies provided these critical data points. By following these steps you will be able to focus on the top issues faced by management.

I.   Determine the members of the team that will oversee the program

Over 50 percent of the time companies create teams to run and monitor the workforce planning initiative. The teams are made up of individuals representing multiple business units, at least one senior executive and HR. Typically the team size is limited to fewer than ten individuals.

The next choice companies favor is to have one full time individual responsible for the program. This choice is favored less than 20% of the time, and 10% of the time the team is only made up of HR.

In addition, the team member from HR will need to dedicate at least half of his/her time to this program. If your organization is large enough, and even more importantly has a global presence, you should consider a creating a new position with the title of *Manager or Director of Workforce Planning*.

The individual selected from HR must have the skills to lead an initiative this large. Those skills include a strong analytic background, excellent communication abilities and an overall knowledge of the organization. This is not a stretch assignment for someone unprepared for such a high profile position. However, it may be considered as a rotational position with a minimum of two year commitment.

Our recommendations include recruiting a senior executive to "champion" the cause and ensure the process stays on-track. The notion of spreading the tentacles of the process throughout the organization aligns with the comprehensive approach. By selecting individuals from the business units to be on the team or taskforce you are spreading the responsibility, and ultimately accountability, for the program across the company.

It is critical that the business units are involved from the beginning. By doing so, you will capture the attention of a wider audience and eventually have access to the resources needed to sustain the process over the long haul.

II. Establish a budget and budgeting protocol

This program will require dedicated resources. The actual amount you will need depends on the size and reach of the organization along with the scope of the workforce planning program.

One of the major flaws in many workforce planning programs that cause the program to have little impact is the lack of a formal budget. It is one of the areas we have had feedback from individuals stating that putting a formal budget in place was something they would do in the future.

For the companies that do have budgets for their programs there are several options they use. The budget process companies' use includes an annual budget review where they submit the needs for the coming year. In some cases companies seek grants and state funding where available. The majority of the time it is included in the overall HR budget and not separated out. Our recommendation is that you begin to create a line item for the HR budget and this program.

There are several reasons for establishing a budget protocol. In our research we observed that companies rarely use a formal budget yet over 50% of the companies in our survey state they have spent over $50,000 in the recent past and will spend $50,000 plus annually going forward. This amount is conservative as some have reported spending easily $100,000 on this program. If the a program is intended to improve efficiency in the company, then the investment should be documented and attached to a set of metrics to track these improvements as a return on investment (ROI).

A dedicated budget requires the team to be accountable for their spending, as well as creating the opportunity for re-allocation from other programs that may not have as much impact on the company.

III. Research and benchmark workforce planning

The opportunities for research and gaining insights on workforce planning are somewhat limited. Not many resources are available which is why we chose to write this **Handbook**. Most companies take advantage of several options of research when they:

✓ Attend conferences or workshops
✓ Purchase books, materials
✓ Conduct benchmarking
✓ Form an exploratory taskforce
✓ Hire consultants
✓ Conduct in-depth research

The majority of the emphasis was placed on attending workshops, conferences and purchasing materials and books on workforce planning.

We recommend going an additional step and have a certified master trainer in workforce planning, our company conducts these certifications. Having a specialist in workforce planning to guide and lead the process sends a message to the entire company. That message is a resolution to the process.

IV. Determine the timeline and pilot group

In our research, 50% of the companies had HR take the lead on the implementation, 33% recruited a senior executive to champion the program, and 42% decided to bring the program on-line very discretely with little fanfare.

As far as the pace and method of implementation goes, that will be dictated by the size and geographical spread of your company. Also, the implementation of a program will change based on your organizational structure.

If you are primarily a decentralized organization with separate business units, select one area and initiate a pilot program. Learn from that process and make changes before moving on to the next one.

If your company is centralized and primarily in one or two locations you will find it easier to institute a comprehensive program by "seeding" each area with a trained and certified individual representing that business area. This way all parts of the company will feel included and able to partake in the implementation.

When it comes to adaptations and improvements, set up the initial evaluation and metrics on a time-line so after the first 90 days there is an opportunity to make changes. Also, with our modular process you will be able to step through each one slowly to ensure it is working.[3]

Design Challenges

Our research has guided us to discover the organizational challenges every organization will face as they begin implementing a workforce planning program. These steps need to be discussed openly with your taskforce or implementation team.

Every time there is an attempt at change, there are organizational challenges. The usual response is for a major "change management" effort focused on crafting methods to motivate individuals and recruit champions to lead the initiative. You will be facing the same "change management" issues when you are considering a workforce planning program.

> **Caution - actions that could undermine your program.**

Our research indicates these benchmarks. When you begin to implement a workforce planning program pay special attention to each one of the following areas:

A. Line managers are resistant or skeptical. Over 60% of the participants indicated the biggest challenge was overcoming the hesitancy of the line managers to participate. They failed to see the long-term benefits and did not express support. Given that the business units are the major players in this program it is important to get them on-board early.

B. Organizational structure impacts collaboration. If your business units are structured in a way that there is little cooperation or communication then this program will be difficult to use. It is critical to have an understanding of competency needs and tie specifics to the talent acquisition and talent development needs for each business unit. If they are reticent to participate then they will not gain the full complement of benefits. Collaboration among business units and centralized functions is imperative for this to have a chance to work.

C. Senior leadership fails to commit a budget or support to the program. This is the most difficult challenge to overcome. If there is little commitment from senior leaders and they do not designate a budget for this program it is doubtful it will succeed. In order to achieve senior leadership buy-in you will need to build a comprehensive business case on the state of your workforce and explain why this process will be a solution.

Once you deliver an insightful "value proposition," and gain the senior leadership as champions of the program, you should be able to attain a budget. Lack of resources will be an issue you do not want to try to overcome at a later date.

D. Model which will transfer across business units and countries. Your taskforce should design a program which will be adaptable for different business units and especially different countries. Having a flexible model which will allow you to craft narrower competency models will allow for each area to be impacted in a more efficient way.

E. Technology platform for analyzing data. One area that needs to be considered is a platform for technology that will encapsulate the data you begin to capture. This can be done relatively simply if you are a small organization. If you are a global enterprise you will want a web-based application to allow greater inputs and ability to capture and analyze the data.

F. Training for the HR leaders, Senior Leaders and Business Unit Leaders. Having a team training or achieving a Master Certification for workforce planning will be necessary to get everyone on the same page. Also, this process will encourage the development of tools and techniques you will need.

G. Keep the scope of the program focused. In order to attain early success, seek pilot areas where you can make an impact. You can use these successes as evidence prior to rolling it out enterprise wide. Selecting a group and training them on the process will help in the assimilation.

H. Target critical roles first. First, determine the pilot area and the business unit where you will begin to use this process. Start at the top by identifying "Key Positions" and competencies. Having a complete process with the critical roles in a key business area will make the implementation easier.

I. Have someone leading the effort. Even though many organizations have teams leading this effort, our research shows that there is a need for a dedicated individual to guide the overall effort. This will be the full-time position and may be an excellent rotational assignment opportunity. [4]

Recommendations for Your Program

Below are a series of recommendations from The Conference Board. This group spent a year on strategic workforce planning and came up with these steps to be aware of.

   A. *Build on previous successes, such as succession planning, or pilot your program in select business units.*
   B. *Seek partners: In many organizations, HR collaborates with Finance, IT, Strategic Planning, Risk Management and or budgeting to develop and conduct the program.*
   C. *Establish definitive and consistent data that will be used company-wide.*
   D. *Create a common language to describe competencies, jobs and other workforce data.*
   E. *Ensure that data on skills and competencies are updated regularly.*
   F. *Adapt workforce planning to different business needs and workforce dynamics within the organization.*
   G. *Make the process and tools simple and user friendly, and adjust the level of granularity in workforce numbers to the audience.*
   H. *Develop HR staff's capabilities and confidence to be effective partners in the process.*
   I. *Use segmentation to focus on the most critical, high-impact jobs and talent.*
   J. *Seek the means and opportunities to use this process to leverage internal talent.*
   K. *Integrate strategic workforce planning with the business planning process.*
   L. *Make business units accountable for delivering against their workforce plans.* [5]

Adaptations and Changes to Existing Programs

Some of the most attention-grabbing consequences in our research were the decisions companies made to change existing HR programs based on key insights from their workforce planning process.

In the HR literature circles, one of the dominant topics written about describes how leaders are challenged by the complexity of doing business in a global market place. It seems leaders are generally challenged by the difficulty of competing across diverse cultural and geographic borders. Everyone should recognize that the challenges being faced today are only going to get more complex and competitive in the future. One proactive response would be to completely re-evaluate the effectiveness of your recruiting, succession planning and training programs. Our workforce planning program gives you that opportunity.

We believe that there will be companies that figure out the formula to compete globally and begin to take advantage of opening of new markets in different environs regardless of the difficulties. On the opposite side of the equation will be those companies who fall victim to their inability respond in a proactive and strategic manner. Invariably, the differences between these two companies may be very small. One of the defining characteristics undoubtedly will be the performance of their employees.

The reason sports franchises spend so much time and money trying to evaluate players is because they realize their ultimate success is in having the right player with the right skills in the right position. To ensure this happens, they will change their recruiting and training programs to remain competitive.

In corporate America, HR programs such as recruiting, succession planning and training evolve and change over time but they are typically improved in singular fashion and not across the board as one system. In our research, we discovered that companies with workforce planning programs have made improvements (figure 4-1) on a much larger scale than the ones without workforce planning programs. It is our interpretation that they seem to considered *workforce planning* as a strategic tool that drives the other programs.

As you read through the **Handbook**, digest the data from our research, and begin to envision your program. Pay particular attention to the changes other companies have made in their HR delivery areas. In our research, companies state they have made changes with over 50% of the participants in our survey making adaptations in the following areas: [6]

- ✓ Developed new training programs to improve KSAs (Knowledge, Skills and Attributes) in our existing workforce.
- ✓ Developed better programs to source talent.
- ✓ Put in better metrics to measure talent acquisition effectiveness.
- ✓ Developed programs intended to improve retention.
- ✓ Developed creative career pathing to motivate individuals to stay with company.

FIGURE 4-1

Areas HR Changed After Workforce Planning

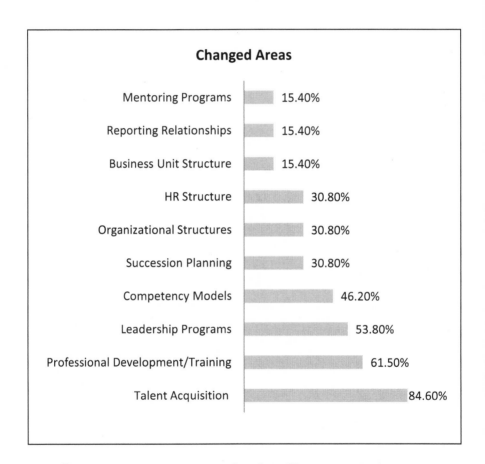

These 10 areas undoubtedly comprise a significant amount of HR programs. Our belief is that these will get better when you use a comprehensive program to evaluate them and how effective they are.

Steps for your taskforce...

In preparation for getting your taskforce on the right page we have designed a list of specific questions to ask and action items for you to do. As each item is reviewed, the buy-in of the group will be enhanced.

Go through each of the following areas. Complete each as needed. Capture the critical competencies and information you will need for the future of your company. These are divided into four sessions. They openly can be discussed at one setting or divided up into several meetings.

Taskforce
Session I

Respond to these questions and share the results with your team members. Document any specific concerns which you feel will make this program more or less successful.

Have you developed a comprehensive set of competencies linked to the business strategy?

_____

_____

_____

_____

_____

_____

_____

_____

Have you determined the quantity and sources of skills required for implementing your strategic business plans for the next five years?

_____

_____

_____

_____

_____

_____

_____

_____

What value will these performance standards deliver to the organization?

_____

_____

_____

_____

_____

_____

_____

_____

Taskforce
Session II

Respond to these questions and share the results with your team members. Document any specific concerns which you feel will make this program more or less successful.

What will be the impact be on the business and overall success of the company if you do not have a strategic workforce plan?

_____

_____

_____

_____

_____

_____

_____

_____

What are the key reasons your company need to
strategically plan for the future?

_____

_____

_____

_____

_____

_____

_____

_____

_____

_____

_____

_____

_____

_____

_____

Taskforce
Session III

Respond to these questions and share the results with your team members. Document any specific concerns which you feel will make this program more or less successful.

Begin to list the individuals you will consider for seeking input on defining the future needs for your organization.

_____

_____

_____

_____

_____

_____

_____

_____

Begin to list the individuals in senior leadership that you will present this program to for approval.

_____

_____

_____

_____

_____

_____

_____

In your opinion, what are the key business areas which will need different skills for the future?

_____

_____

_____

_____

_____

_____

_____

_____

Begin to draft the timeline for conducting focus groups which will reveal your needs for skills in the future.

_____

_____

_____

_____

_____

_____

_____

_____

Taskforce
Session IV

Respond to these questions and share the results with your team members. Document any specific concerns which you feel will make this program more or less successful.

How has your organization handled change in the past?

_____

_____

_____

_____

_____

What are the key issues you will need to resolve before this program can be successful?

_____

_____

_____

_____

_____

_____

Checklist for your organization

Focus requires a process of getting closer to the object you're viewing and it requires a device which will provide clarity from a distance. These checklists are intended to bring clarity to your process and open the door for more customization. Our process is called "lensing-in" which means tightening the view or increasing the power on the microscope to sharpen the image. This is in contrast to companies that "filter-out" areas they believe are unnecessary. The checklists can be used to refine your needs.

*The results will be transferrable to your *90 Day Action Plan*.*

Take the results from the team members and summarize in this checklist.

FIGURE 4-2

Checklist Summary for Taskforce Members

Taskforce	Summarize Needs	Next Steps
Session I		
Session II		
Session III		
Session IV		

This program has to be integrated as a pillar of the corporate strategy. When you do, your ability to forecast solutions will improve.

Part III

Moving From Reaction to Prediction

5. The Work

As history was being lived out, the financial times of 2008 reflected companies that were good, bad and ugly. We witnessed great brand name companies unable to avoid downsizing their workforce just to stay fiscally solvent. Any company fortunate enough to be untouched by the global economic doldrums was in the minority. Lost in this turmoil of panic was the ultimate question. What will our workforce look like if we survive?

This program has answers that will make a difference. In all likelihood, strategic workforce planning is destined to be the HR tool to sustain you in tough times well into the future.

In every organization, there comes a point for change. Our formula for workforce planning allows you to shape those critical issues needed to institute fundamental change. In this module we guide you to define the *vision of the future*. It is an opportunity to imagine what you can become and what your organization will look like.

Why this module is important

The modules in the *90 Day Action Plan* are interrelated and this one starts your workforce planning program by looking first into the future. All other modules follow. It is important for you to get this one right.

The Work takes you on a path to discovery and understanding change. It is a refined lens giving you the ability to see into the future. In this module we have outlined the progression which is intended to be transferable to any organization and it is mirrored in the other modules. Each step in the methodology is a foundation calling for self exploration and insight with an overall consensus arrived at by your taskforce.

Define the Future Worker

For your organization, the future workforce has not been seen. You, however, are tasked with seeing into the next three years and forecasting the needs. Do not sacrifice the specifics for expediency. All aspects of your initiative have to prove their worth and attain a design element worthy of sustaining the model.

As you begin to structure your view of the organization of the future it is absolutely necessary to identify the specific knowledge, skills, attributes (KSAs) and core competencies which make up the fabric of that tapestry. Organizational structures, reporting relationships and sometimes entire business units will be affected as the picture of the future gains clarity.

FIGURE 5-1

Five Program Modules

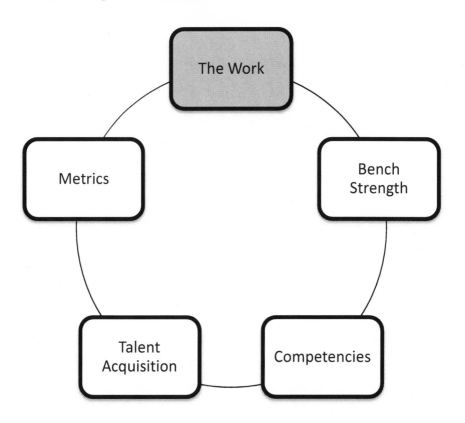

The circular structure of the model deemphasizes hierarchy and highlights the critical nature of the systematic approach. Each interrelated module affects the other and we start you with focusing on defining the fundamentals needed for your company to be successful tomorrow and each day after over the next three years.

> ➤ **How you can use this in your company.**

Organizational change

What distinguishes excellent organizational transformations from run-of-the-mill efforts? Whether they are applied to a business unit or are implemented enterprise wide, an effective transformation is characterized by three important elements; *organizational buy-in, confirmed senior leadership commitment,* and a *long-term view* that the proposed change is necessary for the successful execution of the strategic business objectives. [1]

In the late 1970s the international consulting firm *McKinsey&Company* introduced the *7-S* framework. This watershed paradigm change outlined seven different aspects of organizational change.

> *"A previous focus of managers was on organization as structure that considered who does what, who reports to whom and the like. As organizations grew in size and complexity, the more critical question became one of coordination."* [2]

As we start with this first module called *The Work*, we are turning your attention to the future. In each component in the **Handbook** the individual module is formulated as part of a greater constellation. Just as *McKinsey&Company* dissected the organization with this innovative formula, we believe the paradigm for human capital planning will be re-created with our modular system.

> ## What other companies are doing.

In our benchmark study we asked companies how they felt their workforce planning program would contribute to understanding the future needs of specific KSAs. We note on the chart below 53% of the participants felt their organization's efforts will be ***Very Improved or Extremely Improved*** as they seek to align their KSAs with their future business needs. [3]

FIGURE 5-2

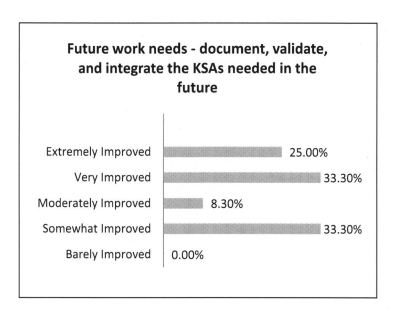

Overview of the Process

One of the most important roles a manager needs to execute is to break down a situation into challenges that team members or subordinates can handle. In essence, by providing clarity and a stage-gate type of progression he/she reduces the ambiguity of the situation and allows the team to function at a higher level of proficiency.

In a focused protocol you will need to examine each step and provide the needed resources. In our overview in these next pages (figure 5-3) we have outlined a series of steps and graphically defined the flow. This flow will change based on your company and its specific needs. (Appendix)

It is a great tool for guiding your taskforce.

> ➤ **How you can use this in your company.**

The tools we have designed are examples which we know will be useful for your organization. Please follow the steps and then customize them for your own needs. They should be excellent starters but are not intended to be used for every organization in the same way.

FIGURE 5-3

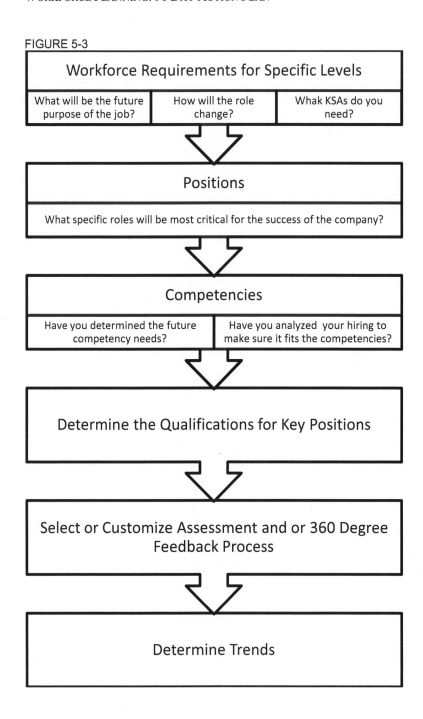

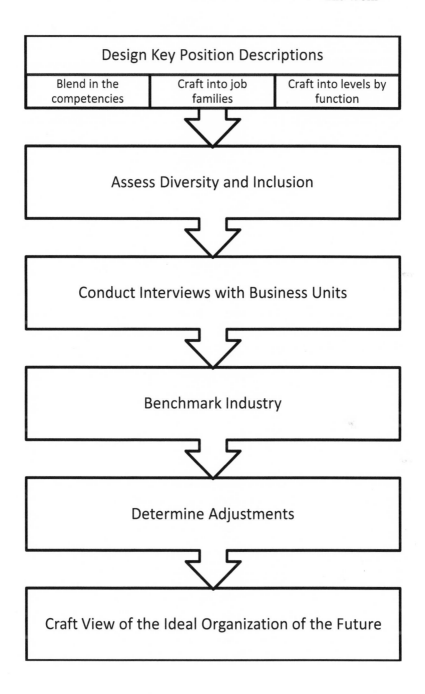

Your Ideal Organization

Instructions

This is an exercise you may choose to incorporate into your *future of the work*. It is an abbreviated version but still gets the point across. Our recommendation is to use this as a base or platform and begin to define a broader range of skills and areas of expertise you will need.

The assessment (figure 5-4) is divided into two sections with the left side listing a series of words and phrases and the right side outlining a scale. Then in the summary, (figure 5-5) we show you how to capture the information on one sheet of data. This series of words and phrases will provide a stepping stone toward defining a workforce planning initiative for your company. Go through the entire list and place a check mark next to the rating for proficiency as you *want it to be.*

In this assessment you are looking for the descriptors, adjectives, adverbs, competencies, skills, attributes and images that describe the final product of a workforce planning program after it is in place and functionally strong.

This section is based on the execution of the work in your organization. As you review each item ask yourself, how important your need is in this area to execute properly and to succeed in the future? The scale is from Low to High need. (Appendix)

FIGURE 5-4

Execution Section I					
KSA for Future	**Low**	**Low to Moderate**	**Moderate**	**Moderate to High**	**High**
Analytical Thinking					
Decision Making					
Financial Management					
Resource Management					
Continuous Improvement					
Creativity					
Collaboration					
Strategic Section II					
KSA for Future	**Low**	**Low to Moderate**	**Moderate**	**Moderate to High**	**High**
Strategic and global mindset					
Translate a vision for the future of a work group					
Building Partnerships					
Strategic Analysis					

Interpersonal Section III					
KSA for Future	**Low**	**Low to Moderate**	**Moderate**	**Moderate to High**	**High**
Accountability					
Adaptability					
Resilience					
Communication					
Stress Tolerance					
Valuing Diversity					
Leadership Section IV					
KSA for Future	**Low**	**Low to Moderate**	**Moderate**	**Moderate to High**	**High**
Initiative					
Integrity					
Judgment					
Implement Plans					
Managing Conflict					
Consult/Advise					
Developing Talent					
Technical Section V					
KSA for Future	**Low**	**Low to Moderate**	**Moderate**	**Moderate to High**	**High**
Technical Solution Development					
Technology Management					

Summarize your findings, compare notes
and plug these findings into your plan.

FIGURE 5-5

KSAs /Competency	Prepared / Not Prepared
Section I	
Section II	
Section III	
Section IV	
Section V	
Overall Areas for Focus	

The Leaders for Our Future

FIGURE 5-6

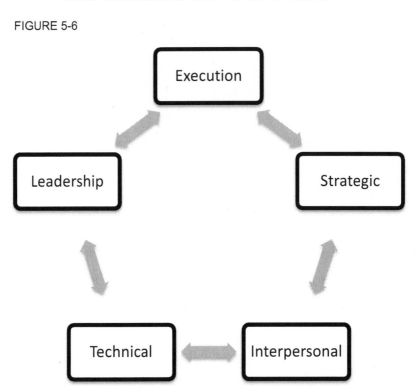

Ownership of a defined, predictive, and impactful model for leadership is important in any organization. The sources and dimensions you use to identify and prepare the successful leaders for your future will depend on your organization's needs as shown in figures 5-5 and 5-6. Our definition is clearly brief but it conveys the concept. We mean "ownership" in the literal term of *it is yours and describes you.* As you take ownership, the process will transform as you begin validating your competencies, structuring a professional development program and strategically aligning your performance management protocol.

> **What other companies are doing.**

In this module we are looking at the future. Here is a list of seven drivers of labor costs from IBM:

1. *Effective Sourcing*
2. *Workforce restructuring*
3. *Subcontractor optimization*
4. *Performance management*
5. *Hiring mix*
6. *Alternate workforce models*
7. *Redeployment*

Of this list IBM identified three that were most influential: *effective sourcing, workforce restructuring, and subcontractor optimization.*

After careful analysis, they used this understanding of costs in labor and strategy to gain insights and make a determination on program direction.[4]

❖ **Take this series of seven drivers of costs and propose that your taskforce come up with the ones that affect your organization.**

Steps for your taskforce...

This is an exercise for your taskforce, leaders, or HR team. It also is a critical component for addressing the current inventory of skills and competencies in your company.

**In addition, you will find exercises and forms to use with your business units in the Appendix of the Handbook. **

In an arch, there is one stone that is shaped differently and it fits directly in the middle of the arch. It is called the "key stone" and it determines the strength of the arch. In our program there are many stones in the arch which we call the modules. This section describes the "key stone" for making your program in workforce planning strategically linked to the business objectives.

The initial steps you will take to design and then implement a strategic workforce planning program include *drilling down* or taking a *deep-dive* with your business unit partners. This part of the process is to define the positions which strategically will be connected to your future organizational success. This process will be woven into the program and included in *The Work* and *Bench Strength* modules.

This diagram highlights the different positions in your organization which are considered key to the strategic success of the company. The levels reflect the positions most important to the mission of the company.

Strategic Segmentation

FIGURE 5-7

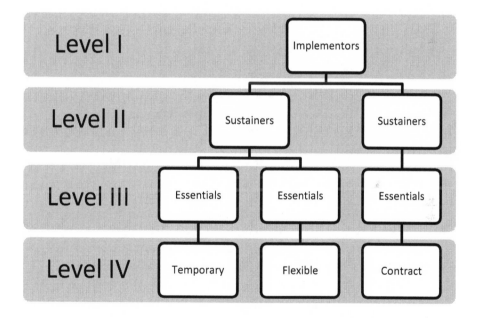

Future Organizational Structure

Individuals in Level I are defined as significantly important and needed for the successful implementation of the strategy. We give them the designation of the *implementers.* They will be the future of the company and its competitive lifeblood.

In most cases this group will make up anywhere from 10% to 20% of your workforce depending on the actual structure, reporting relationships and global or geographic reach of the company. It also will translate to the more important individuals and leadership of the company. It is essential to define the competencies and positions based on the strategic direction of the company. Also, when there is a change in one of these positions, there is a tremendous ripple effect on the organization they influence. More individuals in lower levels will be added or subtracted as this level changes.

We want you to evaluate how this framework can be applied to your organization. Consider each section separately and respond to what it will mean for your company to adopt this organizational view of the future. Don't get bogged down in terminology, although language is important. Once each taskforce member understands the concept and levels of the strategic segmentation you will have the ability to incorporate a radically new organizational structure.

What does this mean for my company?

_____

_____

_____

_____

_____

Future Organizational Structure

Level II individuals and competencies are considered significant, but less so than the implementation and a part of the core of the sustaining effort of the strategy.

This group of **sustainers** may make up another 10% to 20% depending on the organization. They are the conduit and measuring level in the organization. They oversee the implementation, make course correction, measure and are accountable for the success of portions of the strategy as they share in the overall success of the process.

What does this mean for my company?

_____

_____

_____

_____

_____

_____

Future Organizational Structure

Level III individuals and competencies are **_essentials_** to the execution of the strategy. They make up 20% to 40% of your workforce. These individuals are the actuators and are responsible for the delivery of the programs and processes needed to be successful. They execute, bring a competitive advantage to the success of the strategy and make up the future leadership of the company.

Level IV individuals and competencies are considered more readably replaceable and can fluctuate and change based on the direction and strategy. It is an area made up of **contract** workers, **temporary** individuals or flexible teams which are defined by the need. It is an important part of the organizational structure because it is the most flexible one. They make up 20% to 40% of your workforce. The actual number will be dictated by the type of work and method of going to market. Many companies have large projects which drive their business and to have possibly 50% or more flex workers would not be unusual.

What does this mean for my company?

_____

_____

_____

_____

_____

Define a Key Position for your company...

If you had a pre-conceived notion of a key position, has it changed after you experienced the exercises? Has it changed after conversing with your taskforce? Plug these findings into your plan.

_____

_____

_____

_____

Strategic Communication Tools

For each of the four levels in our Strategic Segmentation platform you will need to partner with the business units to understand the future and present. This format is a guided discussion tool. It is to be used by the taskforce, trainers, and HR as they meet with the business leaders for decoding the needs. This is an example. There is a separate format for each level. (Appendix)

What roles are critical to driving the long-term strategic advantage for your business?

Describe your needs:

What impact will they have on the top-line growth?

Describe your needs:

What impact will they have on our overall strategic direction?

Describe your needs:

How will these roles give our company a competitive advantage over the competition?

Describe your needs:

When it comes to calculating the fulfilling of these roles will it be to our advantage to seek to acquire these individuals or to train someone in the company?

Action Plan:

Checklist for your organization

The next step for your taskforce is to decipher specific needs and set an agenda. The results will be transferrable to your *90 Day Action Plan.*

FIGURE 5-8

Taskforce Objectives	Summarize Needs	Next Steps
Ideal Organization		
Five Sections for Leaders		
KSAs for Future		
Communication Tools		
Cautions		
Key Position		
Strategic Segmentation		
Principles Applied		

*In strong economies a
recession seems far off. It
is impossible to predict the
next economic downturn.
This section makes sure
you know where you stand
in your human capital just
as you need to do in your
financial capital.*

Part IV

Setting
the Standard
Today

6. Bench Strength

At this point in the *90 Day Action Plan* your workforce planning implementation should be in full swing. Let's take a step back and understand how far you have come. You have established *need* and built a sound *business case* for your organization. Then you identified and recruited the taskforce and gained the commitment of the senior leaders along with a budget. Next, you crafted a compelling and focused image of the workforce need for the future and tied this image to a validated and defined competency model. Now we are in search of the methods and techniques to decipher the mystery of your current workforce. This area called your *Bench Strength* represents the largest and most accessible inventory of talented individuals capable of successfully executing the business strategy. It is critical for you to determine where you are and set the *standard today* for the *success of the future.*

*B*ench *Strength* is defined as the current employee population. We have separated this module into critical aspects which are important to the definition of a healthy organization. In this chapter we discuss:

➢ Career Pathing
➢ Competencies
➢ Competitiveness
➢ Diagnosing Needs
➢ Key Positions
➢ Measuring
➢ Organizational Design
➢ Performance Management
➢ Professional Development
➢ Replacement Policy
➢ Succession Planning

Why this module is important

The modules in the *90 Day Action Plan* are interrelated. The *Bench Strength* emphasizes the current workforce. We want to caution you to be careful and not misinterpret this section or it will be poorly implemented. The tendency may be to assume you have thought-out the necessary HR delivery mechanisms including professional development, succession planning, performance management and career pathing and are ready to go. You will be initiating a new process that is more strategic. We would like to carefully walk through several areas to focus on. These steps make this module work.

➢ Conduct a comprehensive inventory of skills and competencies in your current workforce.

> ➢ Determine the quantity of existing competencies by level when overlaid on the segmentation model.

> ➢ Validate the competency model by comparing it against the performance management scores in the existing employee base.

> ➢ Compare the results from the promotions over the last two years against the current set of standards required. Did you promote the right individuals? How would you improve in the future?

> ➢ Proactively create your human capital strategy in annual increments by setting goals for one through five years. What competencies and KSAs do you need but don't have? What is the plan to capture them?

> ➢ Measure the sustainable results for your program by incorporating the metrics needed to ensure a balanced approach.

In the theater, at the beginning of a play, the director and producer hold a "casting call." There is an announcement to the general acting population for the needs of the production as far as each role and the number of actors required. During these tryouts a director looks for how an actor interprets or translates the believability of the written part in the play so the audience can relate to and enjoy the production. The director will select a "lead" and an "understudy" for each critical role. In a sense, the long standing tradition of requiring an individual to be available to step in to the role can be seen as evidence of workforce planning. The director does not want to chance the play being unsuccessful for even one performance; so he ensures the seamless transition of a replacement actor in case the lead actor is unable to perform.

What makes this comparison with corporate America so intriguing is how efficiently theatrical productions incorporate these workforce planning techniques. Casting calls are the company equivalent of job fairs and recruiting extravaganzas. In corporate America the hiring managers replace the producers and directors. They use behavioral based interviewing and other types of "realistic job previews" attempting to find out what type of person is needed for the role they are seeking to fill in their company.

In a company a character or as human resources prefer, *characteristics,* end up being equally important as the hiring manager attempts to know the make-up, personality, appropriate experience and temperament of the person. If a company had designated understudies when someone leaves, or is unable to perform the particular role, there would be a suitable substitute to take over and ensure the ongoing success of the program or business enterprise.

This comparison brings a valid question to your company. Do you treat the current cast the same way you approach finding outsiders? Why not hold a "casting call" inside your company?

In the past;

> ***"Succession planning and management activities focused on leaders at the top of organizational hierarchies because organizations were controlled from the top down ... But times have changed. Few organizations have the luxury to overstaff in the face of fierce competition from abroad."*** [1]

FIGURE 6-1

Five Program Modules

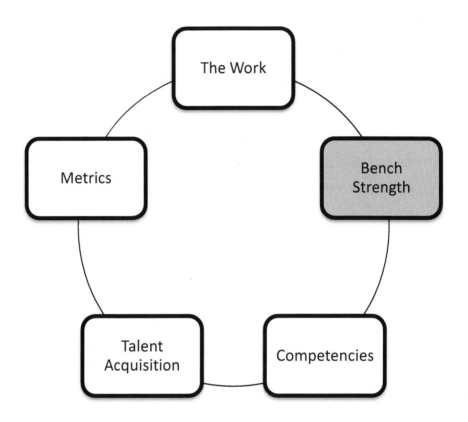

Many companies fall short when it comes to utilizing people measures that are linked directly to the business strategy. By that we mean, incorporating an evaluation of effectiveness and efficiency that measures programs on the human side of the business as they directly correlate to the improvement and success of the operations side of the business.

For example, in this module, we are discussing the depth of the competencies and skills available in your current employee population to execute the business strategy for the next five years. Bench strength is made up of the performers and players who not only execute the business today but are the resource for the future leadership of the company. This area is where you invest the most money and look to make the most impact. The two programs delivered by HR when it comes to bench strength are training and succession planning.

How do you measure the effectiveness and efficiency in your training and succession planning programs?

In their study published in an article by McKinsey&Company called *Anatomy of a Healthy Corporation*, authors DeSmet, Loch, and Schainger, define the attributes of a health organization as being *Resilience, Execution, Alignment, Renewal, and Complimentary* concepts. Each of these characteristics relates to how competitive an organization can become. By examining a strategic link between these attributes and defining each as an organizational requirement, you can begin to calibrate your training and succession planning programs for effectiveness and efficiency.[2]

The McKinsey&Company study describes the following aspects of healthy corporations.

Resilience is evidenced in a company by the ability to rebound from a problem and have a strong planning process anticipating market fluctuations or even the impact of a natural disaster like hurricane Katrina. Utilizing an assessment tool such as a 360 degree feedback process, the same attribute can be observed and documented in an individual.

Execution can be described as the ability to make sound and timely decisions as evidenced in the ability to forecast for the future as well as having employees who understand their roles and responsibilities.

Alignment is achieved as companies define a compelling vision of the future, connect all of the employees and articulate a shared identity that rises above functions and business units as they reinforce a sense of common purpose.

Renewal is seen when a company leverages a particular set of competencies to facilitate the foray into a new market arena. It is also reflected in how companies will reinvent a product or service area as their own through the fundamentals they have in their own culture.

Complimentary concept is described through the book by John Roberts called *The Modern Firm* and expands on how a company will hire, train, promote and develop its employees with a set of mutually reinforcing behaviors. Often Toyota is singled out as a company that strives to build capacity and management systems into everything they do.

The authors additionally related that, "executives must imbed healthy thinking in formal people-management mechanisms, including performance contracts, incentives, career path planning and staffing decisions." [3]

Can you begin to envision a particular set of attributes used to describe your company? Are they reflective of a healthy organization? Can you relate to this group of adjectives from the study describing a healthy corporation?

Once you determine the core attributes, or competency model for your organization, you can begin to assess how healthy your company is. It is possible that you feel the attributes determined to be important in the McKinsey&Company study are important to you or that others are more appropriate.

> ## What other companies are doing.

When it comes to taking your HR programs to the next level it may help you to understand what other companies are doing. In our research we have found that companies that seek to embed the critical concepts of workforce planning have anticipated improvements in their HR programs.

Workforce planning will give your organization the opportunity to impact multiple programs at one time because the plan is focused on one result and that is the success of the business. Companies that are executing this process have already experienced this phenomenon of improvements in multiple areas of HR.

We asked each company in our study the following question with regards to Succession Planning, Performance Management and Professional Development.

As a result of your workforce planning program how much improvement do you anticipate in each of these areas?

This series of charts point out what we mean. Each one describes a specific part of the *Bench Strength* module and the scores show the percent of the surveyed audience that anticipates improvement. 4 In figures 6-2 through 6-4 we highlight their responses.

FIGURE 6-2

102

FIGURE 6-3

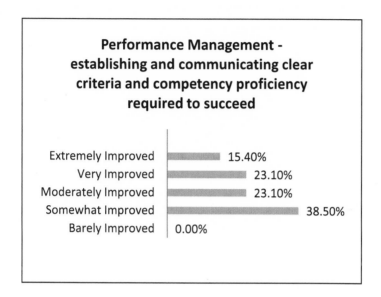

**Performance Management -
establishing and communicating clear
criteria and competency proficiency
required to succeed**

Extremely Improved	15.40%
Very Improved	23.10%
Moderately Improved	23.10%
Somewhat Improved	38.50%
Barely Improved	0.00%

FIGURE 6-4

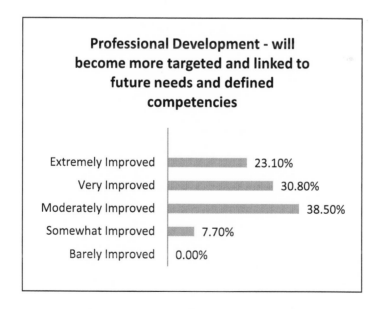

**Professional Development - will
become more targeted and linked to
future needs and defined
competencies**

Extremely Improved	23.10%
Very Improved	30.80%
Moderately Improved	38.50%
Somewhat Improved	7.70%
Barely Improved	0.00%

Define Your Key Positions

Key positions in your organization are the ones which you need to create the strategy and execute it. They are the critical roles which have been identified by technical skills, organizational position, core competencies, or other criteria. Key positions underscore and emphasize important work processes that must be carried out for the organization to achieve its strategic objectives.

Key positions will leverage points in the organization affecting critical success milestones or foundational objectives without which the overall accomplishment of these objectives is not possible. They mostly are viewed with a long-term lens.

> *"The workforce is generally regarded as one of the keys – if not the key – to an organization's success. An effective HR policy is one of the keystones of corporate strategy, and some even regard it as the cornerstone."* [5]

Competency-Based Bench Strength

For individuals in key positions it is easy to relate to sports teams. Good coaches know the strengths and weaknesses of the players on their bench, and they don't get caught short when it comes time to make a substitution. Organizations would do well to follow suit.

A competency-based succession planning system allows a company to assess its bench strength using predetermined criteria linked to the business strategy and validated against performance measures. Individual and aggregate assessments of competency levels and relevant behaviors can help identify the presence or absence of key capabilities at an organizational level. [6]

Define a Key Position in your company...

_____

_____

_____

_____

_____

_____

> ## How you can use this in your company.

Assessments Become Necessary

It is critical in workforce planning to diagnose and understand the results of organizational preparedness to become more competitive. It is important to assess the skills, key players, development criteria and competitive advantages or disadvantages you may have. As a first step in predicting key positions, take a look at an organizational analysis. It is a systematic process of examining how an organization is positioned to address future challenges. It can also be understood as an effort to assess an organization's strengths and weaknesses. Ask the following questions:

❖ How well positioned is the organization presently to respond to effects of future trends?

❖ What action steps can the organization take to meet the threats and opportunities posed by future trends?

❖ How can the organization maximize its strengths and minimize its weaknesses as the future unfolds in the present?

❖ What are the changes you need for the organization in structure and alignment?

❖ What are the work processes you need to evaluate and who are the leaders in these key areas to partner with? [7]

Diagnosing is Important

In any organization, problem solving is an important skill. Too much time can be spent on the proverbial "putting out fires" which are simply quick and easy problems to solve. What many organizations are not very good at is the "identification" of the right problems they should be addressing. If a surgeon incorrectly identifies a part of someone's body that doesn't need surgery he may incorrectly damage or remove that part. Therefore a surgeon uses multiple views, opinions, tools and methods for diagnosing.

In the book on developing leaders called *The Leadership Pipeline*, the authors agree on the importance of diagnosing and understanding where you are. They found that just about every organization has people working at the wrong leadership levels. Why is it important to diagnose these problems? Why can a company still thrive if its leaders are working at the wrong levels but still deliver results? They state three compelling reasons:

1. Important work isn't getting done even though there is a significant amount of output.
2. The cost of each business transaction is increased.
3. People don't develop properly.

This insidious chain reaction can't be stopped without proper diagnosis. Only when the cause of the problem is located and spelled out can a solution be implemented. [8]

Overview of the Process

To understand your *Bench Strength* you can use a variety of tools and techniques.

- ➤ Identify what a healthy organization looks lie to you.
- ➤ Link succession planning to performance management and professional development programs.
- ➤ Define your key positions.
- ➤ Utilize competency based criteria for hiring, development, and succession planning.
- ➤ Assess for organizational preparedness to compete.
- ➤ Diagnose for overall effectiveness of your current workforce.

In our overview in these next pages we have outlined a series of steps and graphically defined the flow (figure 6-5). This exercise is similar to the process you went through in *The Work* (Future) module. You will need to examine each step and consider how your organization fits in these areas. This flow will change based on your company and its specific needs. (Appendix)

FIGURE 6-5

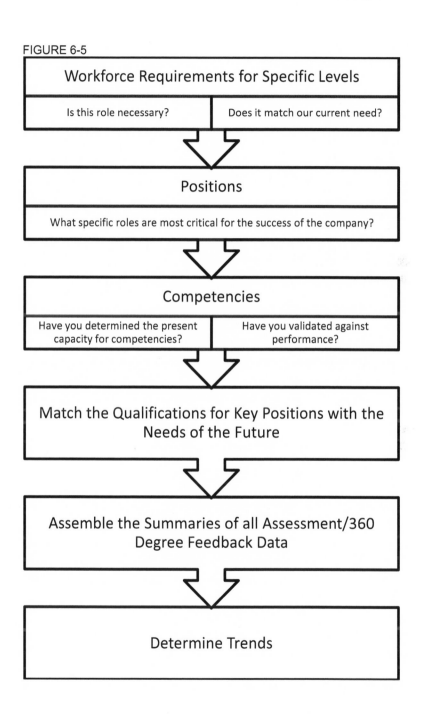

Workforce Requirements for Specific Levels

| Is this role necessary? | Does it match our current need? |

Positions

What specific roles are most critical for the success of the company?

Competencies

| Have you determined the present capacity for competencies? | Have you validated against performance? |

Match the Qualifications for Key Positions with the Needs of the Future

Assemble the Summaries of all Assessment/360 Degree Feedback Data

Determine Trends

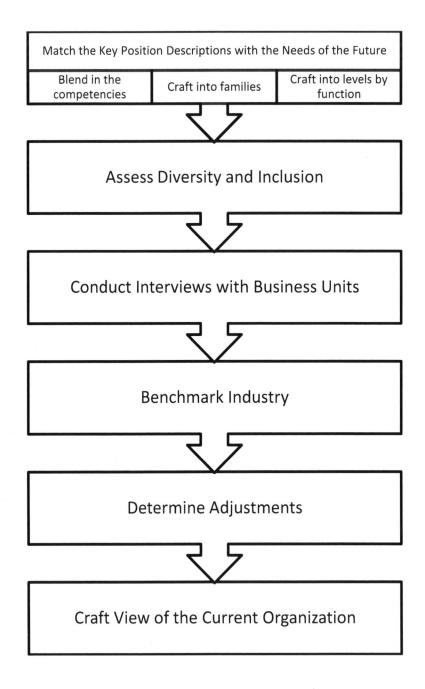

Steps for your taskforce...

This is an exercise for your taskforce, leaders, or HR team. It also is a critical component for addressing the current inventory of skills and competencies in your company.

Focus on Diagnosing Your Workforce

This *sample exercise* is an introduction to areas you will need to consider. The balance of skills and competencies in the leaders for your future will determine the other levels you will need to be competitive.

These five areas are not the only ones you may want to evaluate but they are a start. If you have never assessed these needs then this grouping will get you on your way for the first 30 days of your program.

There are many tools and competency levels you can choose to consider. Start small and build as you see the need. Above all keep the focus tighter than broader because a diluted and poorly designed image of the leadership will keep you from customizing your program.

*Although this exercise is an abbreviated version it still gets the point across. Our recommendation is to use this as a base or platform and begin to define a broader range of skills and expertise areas you currently have. *

The assessment is divided into two sections with the left side listing a series of words and phrases and the right side outlining a scale. Each word or phrase will provide a stepping stone toward defining a workforce planning initiative for your company. Go through the entire list and place a check mark next to the rating for proficiency as you currently see your organization.

> ➤ **How you can use this in your company.**

The tools we have designed are examples which we know will be useful for your organization. Please follow the steps and then customize them for your own needs. They should be excellent starters but are not intended to be used for every organization in the same way.

This section is based on the execution of the work in your organization. As you review each item ask yourself, how prepared are we with our current skills and attributes? The scale emphasizes from Low to High degree of preparedness. (Appendix)

FIGURE 6-6

Execution Section I					
KSA for Future	**Low**	**Low to Moderate**	**Moderate**	**Moderate to High**	**High**
Analytical Thinking					
Decision Making					
Financial Management					
Resource Management					
Continuous Improvement					
Creativity					
Collaboration					
Strategic Section II					
KSA for Future	**Low**	**Low to Moderate**	**Moderate**	**Moderate to High**	**High**
Strategic and global mindset.					
Translate a vision for the future of a work group.					
Building Partnerships					
Strategic Analysis					

Interpersonal Section III					
KSA for Future	**Low**	**Low to Moderate**	**Moderate**	**Moderate to High**	**High**
Accountability					
Adaptability					
Resilience					
Communication					
Stress Tolerance					
Valuing Diversity					

Leadership Section IV					
KSA for Future	**Low**	**Low to Moderate**	**Moderate**	**Moderate to High**	**High**
Initiative					
Integrity					
Judgment					
Implement Plans					
Managing Conflict					
Consult/Advise					
Developing Talent					

Technical Section V					
KSA for Future	**Low**	**Low to Moderate**	**Moderate**	**Moderate to High**	**High**
Technical Solution Development					
Technology Management					

Summarize your findings and compare notes. Then plug these findings into your plan.

KSAs /Competency	Prepared / Not Prepared
Section I	
Section II	
Section III	
Section IV	
Section V	
Overall Areas for Focus	

FIGURE 6-7

Bench Strength
Leadership Potential

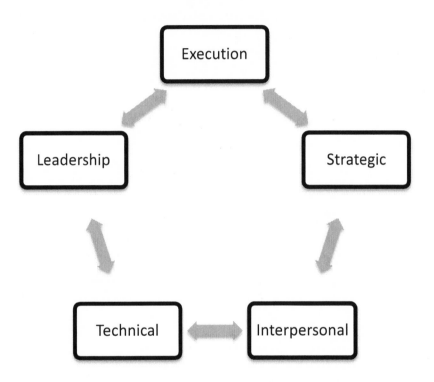

Does your potential reflect your need?
Where will you start to create your
new company?

> **Caution – actions that could undermine your program.**

In the next section we discuss the need for a *replacement policy*. For this program to work, all of these recommendations are to be implemented only after carefully reviewing your current policies and procedures and adhering to all appropriate legal requirements.

When the Gate Opens

Retention takes perseverance and determination. It is always surprising to us when a leader in a company becomes upset when one of his/her key subordinates leaves the company. It is as though the figurative gate has been left open and one of the *prize sheep* has drifted away from the *fold*. If that image resonates then one has to wonder, "Why was the *gate* closed in the first place?"

> **How you can use this in your company.**

The tools we have designed are examples which we know will be useful for your organization. Please follow the steps and then customize them for your own needs. They should be excellent starters but are not intended to be used for every organization in the same way.

Replacement Policy

The first requirement is that the "key position" criteria have been determined and this role fulfills at least 80% of the criteria.

The individual has left the company voluntarily and this not considered part of a re-organization.

The Replacement Policy Model outline follows a series of questions:

> Is the position located in a primary business unit?
>> a. If *no* then leave the position open for 90 days to determine the need to replace.
>> b. If *yes* then go to the next step.

> Is there a developed pipeline from which a clear candidate slate is identified?
>> a. If *yes* then proceed to following your selection process.
>> b. If *no* then proceed to the next step.

> Is the position a leadership role responsible for four or more subordinates?
>> a. If *no* and only one to three individuals are impacted then re-distribute these individuals into a supporting structure that fits the need.
>> b. If *yes* then move to the next step.

> Can this group be considered strong enough to become a team?
>> a. If *yes* then initiate team training.
>> b. If *no* then move to the next step.

> Can the entire area be absorbed into another business group?
> > a. If *yes* then begin the interview and selection process to fit and re-align.
> > b. If *no* then move to the next step.

> Has this business area been re-organized in the last 12 months?
> > a. If *yes*, can the business area return to the previous structure and maintain productivity?
> > b. If *yes* re-align the business and communicate the changes.
> > c. If *no* then go to the next step.

> Initiate the steps required to seek an individual from outside the organization. (Appendix)

Define the replacement policy in your company...

_____

_____

_____

_____

_____

_____

Current Organizational Structure

Following the process from the future work section, consider and document your current organizational structures and challenges in light of the proposed structure and its four levels.

Level I individuals and competencies are defined as significantly important and necessary for the successful implementation of the strategy. The ***implementers*** will be the future of the company and its competitive lifeblood.

In most cases this group will make up anywhere from 10% to 20% of your workforce depending on the actual structure, reporting relationships and global or geographic reach of the company. It also will translate to the more important individuals and leadership of the company. Also, when there is a change in one of these positions, there is a tremendous ripple effect on the organization they control. More individuals in lower levels will be added or subtracted as this level changes.

What does this mean for my company?

_____

_____

_____

_____

_____

Current Organizational Structure

Level II individuals and competencies also are considered significant but less so than the implementation and a part of the core of the sustaining effort of the strategy.

This group of **sustainers** may make up another 10% to 20% depending on the organization. They are the conduit and measuring level in the organization. They oversee the implementation, make course correction, measure and are accountable for the success of portions of the strategy as they share in the overall success of the process.

What does this mean for my company?

_____

_____

_____

_____

_____

_____

_____

Current Organizational Structure

Level III individuals and competencies are ***essentials*** to the execution of the strategy. They make up 20% to 40% of your workforce. These individuals are the actuators and are responsible for the delivery of the programs and processes needed to be successful. They execute, bring a competitive advantage to the success of the strategy and make up the future leadership of the company.

Level IV individuals and competencies are considered more readably replaceable and can fluctuate and change based on the direction and strategy. It is an area made up of **contract** workers, **temporary** individuals or flexible teams which are defined by the need. It is an important part of the organizational structure because it is the most flexible one. They make up 20% to 40% of your workforce. The actual number will be dictated by the type of work and method of going to market. Many companies have large projects which drive their business and to have possibly 50% or more flex workers would not be unusual.

What does this mean for my company?

_____

_____

_____

_____

_____

Strategic Segmentation

FIGURE 6-8

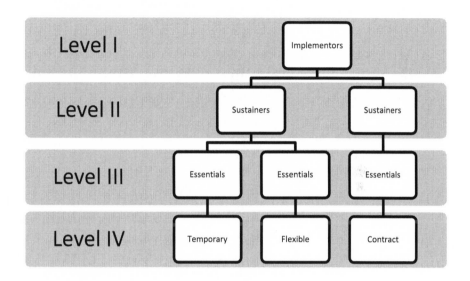

Level I	Implementors
Level II	Sustainers / Sustainers
Level III	Essentials / Essentials / Essentials
Level IV	Temporary / Flexible / Contract

Will this fit in our plan?

_____

_____

_____

_____

Strategic Communication Tools

For each of the four levels in our Strategic Segmentation platform you will need to partner with the business units to understand the future and present. This format is a guided discussion tool. It is to be used by the taskforce, trainers, and HR as they meet with the business leaders for decoding the needs. The comprehensive set of these tools is found in the Appendix.

What roles are critical to driving the long-term strategic advantage for your business?

Describe your needs:

What impact will they have on the top-line growth?

Describe your needs:

What impact will they have on the overall company strategic direction?

Describe your needs:

Action Plan:

How will these roles give the company a competitive advantage over the competition?

Action Plan:

When it comes to calculating the fulfilling of these roles will it be to your advantage to seek to acquire these individuals or to train someone in the company?

Action Plan: (Appendix)

Define a Key Position for your company...

Has it changed after you experienced the exercises? Has it changed after conversing with your taskforce? Plug these findings into your plan.

_____

_____

_____

_____

_____

_____

> How you can use this in your company.

Go through each of these areas and consider what will need improvement. These can be great for delivering a presentation to the senior leadership.

FIGURE 6-9
Summary for Bench Strength Needs

Key Area	Our Status	Improvement
Career Pathing		
Competencies		
Competitive Edge		
Diagnosing Needs		
Key Positions		
Measuring		
Organizational Design		
Performance Management		
Professional Development		
Replacement Policy		
Succession Planning		

Checklist for your organization

The next step for your taskforce is to decipher specific needs and set an agenda for the program. The checklists can be used to refine your needs. The results will be transferrable to your *90 Day Action Plan*. Take the results from the team members and summarize in this checklist.

FIGURE 6-10
Summary Checklist

Taskforce Objectives	Summarize Needs	Next Steps
Five Sections for Leaders		
KSAs for Current		
Communication Tools		
Cautions		
Key Position		
Replacement Policy		

It is imperative that your competencies match the needs of the business. When competencies are strategically aligned, your talent acquisition program will become a competitive advantage.

Part V

Sustaining the Program

7. Competencies

Why competencies are important

In this time of fluidity and change, competency models provide a tool for determining exactly what skills are required to meet the demands of the market as well as providing a venue to express what it takes to be a leader in your organization. A competency model is a highly effective method of communicating the success criteria for both selection of new candidates and the promotion of internal candidates. The individuals understand where they should be striving to improve.

Many different methods of determining a competency model have evolved with the best ones sharing common points. They all lead to identifying superior performance. In addition, competencies are frequently used in conjunction with a variety of assessment tools including 360 degree feedback assessments and behavioral based interviewing protocols for hiring purposes.

In order for competencies to mean something they need to be sound, validated for your organization and predict performance. In addition, the characteristics used are the ones the senior leaders have determined will ultimately prove to be keys to the execution of the strategic objectives.

Using a competency structured process in selecting, hiring and talent development strategies will significantly aid in your organization's ability to predict and forecast the individuals who will be successful and most likely make an impact in your company.

The prediction and forecasting is around the "potential" an individual will exhibit for success in the organization. The cost savings in turn-over and lost production as a result of selection mistakes is easily worth the upfront investment and time.

What is the future of competencies?

What role does a predictive competency model play in the success of your human capital structure? Where does the future lead? In the future, competency modeling approaches are most likely going to focus on long-term organizational fit instead of short-term job matching content and position descriptions. We also feel that companies will put more effort and pay higher attention to criteria in designating key positions and define the larger framework of organizational competencies. The real impact will be for organizations to have customized, specific, measurable, business linked competencies which are validated and sustainable.

FIGURE 7-1

Five Program Modules

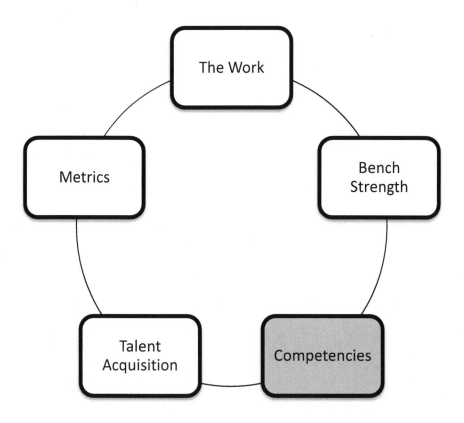

To ensure your competency model reflects your business strategy and enhances the predictive capabilities of your succession planning process, you must scientifically validate the competencies against pre-determined criteria.

According to the study by Jeffrey Shippmann in 2000, the majority of companies fail to develop a robust process for designing their competencies. [1]

➢ Caution – actions that could undermine your program.

As you develop your competencies there are several criteria you should follow to ensure they reflect your business needs. The study conducted by Shippmann was seeking to understand how companies determine their competencies. They use the following set of criteria:

✓ What was the source and method used for crafting the competencies?
✓ Was there a consistency in the type of competency developed?
✓ What were the processes used in developing them?
✓ How detailed were the competencies?
✓ Did they link them to the business goals?
✓ Was there a process for revising and confirming content?
✓ Did they rank each competency or category for importance?
✓ Did the company assess the category or items to determine the reliability of how the competency predicts performance?
✓ Did the company set criteria for each item or category?
✓ Did the company establish a protocol for documenting the process and tracking changes?

This list follows a robust and scientific methodology in securing the correct competencies. Don't panic if you find your company didn't follow this outline of steps. The Shippmann study emphasized that the major problems that companies had included, not properly selecting competencies that would match their needs, not validating the reliability of the competencies and not separating the competencies and creating a hierarchy of ranking for importance.[2]

The reason we have included competencies as a critical part of the program is that they provide the ability to measure and quantify the soft-skill areas in your workforce. Without measures and quantified sets of competencies, workforce planning can become just another HR program. It will be open to critical responses based purely on subjective commentary. In most companies, convincing the business leaders to adopt a new enterprise-wide program is extremely difficult. Measuring your program with the correct metrics and using a robust process of competency modeling will help you to overcome these objections and implement a more successful program.

Competency Modeling Explored

Competency models can provide a comprehensive connection by:

- ✓ Increasing the likelihood of hiring people who will succeed
- ✓ Minimize the investment in people who don't meet expectations
- ✓ Ensure a more systematic interview process
- ✓ Help delineate trainable competencies
- ✓ Focus development on behaviors and skills that matter
- ✓ Ensures training alignment
- ✓ Framework for communications on performance issues
- ✓ Makes a shared understanding on the performance objectives and behaviors sought in leaders

FIGURE 7-2

Our Competency Model

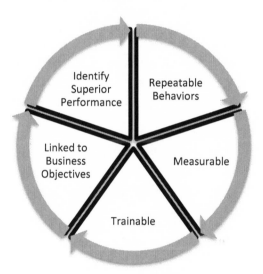

In designing our competency model we have incorporated the definitive aspects of what competencies need to be. As you develop yours, then validate them against recognized standards, keep in mind they need to be customized and meet the following criteria. Competencies have to be understood and written as *repeatable behaviors, measurable, trainable, linked to business objectives* and *capable of identifying the difference between superior performance and average performance.*

> ## What other companies are doing.

In our benchmark study we found companies focused on the interrelated qualities improving their competency model and workforce planning program as strongly predictive for their future success. We were pleased to see 53.9% of the participants felt their organization's efforts will be **Very Improved** *as* they seek to align their competencies with their future business needs. Going one level lower in the survey responses brings the improvement to over 90%.[3]

FIGURE 7-3

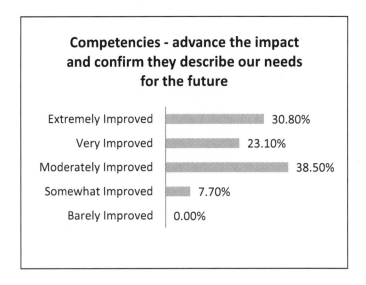

Competencies - advance the impact and confirm they describe our needs for the future

Extremely Improved	30.80%
Very Improved	23.10%
Moderately Improved	38.50%
Somewhat Improved	7.70%
Barely Improved	0.00%

In the U.S. Air Force, using a competency model is a critical part of their succession planning core process. They have used general competencies for a long time and found them useful tools in their HR practice areas. More recently, they have raised the bar of getting promoted by customizing specific competencies for each core process defined by technical needs.

After a core competency requirement has been established for a particular technical specialty such as Munitions, Air Vehicles, or Space Vehicles, the criteria is matched by individuals seeking to transfer or promote in these areas. These individuals are given opportunities in cross-function areas to develop these competencies and advance in their career. By using this approach they are developing a more balanced and higher-proficiency workforce. 4

Improve Predictive Values

By using scientifically developed and validated competencies you will increase the predictive value of your performance management and succession planning processes.

Research brings evidence that high-performers in your current system may not meet the advanced criteria when competencies are incorporated into the evaluation matrix used to determine leadership readiness. 5

As organizations seek to improve their "hit rate" for talent acquisition, succession planning, and overall performance management tools they are increasingly looking for a "bellwether" point on which to capitalize. Competencies, when properly developed and validated against set criteria for your business model, could be the solution you are seeking.

Steps for your taskforce...

This is an exercise for your taskforce, leaders, or HR team. It also is a critical component for addressing the current inventory of skills and competencies in your company.

Respond to these questions and share the results with your team members. Document any specific concerns which you feel will make this program more or less successful.

- ✓ What was the source and method used for crafting our competencies?
- ✓ Was there a consistency in the type of competency developed and did we set criteria for each item or category?

_____

_____

_____

_____

_____

_____

_____

Respond to these questions and share the results with your team members. Document any specific concerns which you feel will make this program more or less successful.

- ✓ How detailed were our competencies and did we link them to our business goals?
- ✓ Was there a process for revising and confirming content?

Respond to these questions and share the results with your team members. Document any specific concerns which you feel will make this program more or less successful.

✓ Did we rank each competency or category for importance?

✓ Did we assess the category or items to determine the reliability of how the competency predicts performance?

✓ Have we set criteria for each item or category and establish a protocol for documenting the process and tracking changes?

_____

_____

_____

_____

_____

_____

_____

Outline the needs you have for enhancing your competency model.

_____

_____

_____

_____

_____

_____

_____

_____

8. Talent Acquisition

In the movie *Men in Black (MIB) Agent K,* the character played by Tommy Lee Jones, hears about the exploits of the character played by Will Smith who has just chased an alien through the streets of New York City. *Agent K* is intrigued by this New York City policeman and identifies him as a possible recruit for the MIB.

In the early scenes from the movie we catch a glimpse of the recruiting process used by the MIB organization. Their methodology employs techniques used by any high performing talent acquisition department; identification, attraction, selection and acquiring the best "fit" for the organization. Even the screening and assessment protocol mirrors a normal company.

Apparently talent acquisition is instrumental even when it comes to monitoring and detaining aliens. In this fictional case, the Will Smith character impresses the MIB with his uncanny instincts. Their criteria included a competency model based on the ability to find and catch aliens. He gets selected as the hiring manager claims, "he chased down a cephalopod and that's good enough for me." [1]

Even though this fantasy adventure captures our imagination with the clever writing and satirical indictment on our conventional behaviors, the script doesn't matter unless the new recruit is identified and acquired.

Why talent acquisition is important to workforce planning

Every organization needs a high-performing talent acquisition group. In this module we focus on why it plays such an important part in our workforce planning program. Our emphasis will be on the recruiters' role in workforce planning. We will not dig into the tools which are part of the technology used in the recruiting groups in most companies. The reason is, we have found little empirical evidence validating significant enhancement to talent acquisition by the addition of a web-based applicant tracking system.

Where is the empirical evidence that a talent applicant tracking system is the most effective method of recruiting? It doesn't exist because the entire premise is based on securing more candidates not better candidates. On the contrary, there is a plethora of scientific evidence that high-performing recruiters do make a difference in identifying, attracting and hiring the best most sought-after candidates.

In addition, when there are economic down-turns and the recruiting efforts slow down, the capital investment sits and gathers dust as the monthly retainer/subscription fees keep coming in. As in 2008, during the downturn economic cycle resulting in historic levels of companies cutting back, having an expensive applicant-tracking system appears ill-conceived and a bad investment.

The only true solution is using a workforce planning program which will adapt and flex with the business needs.

In their book, *Mobilizing Minds*, Lowell Bryan and Claudia Joyce explore options to consider acquiring and retaining the "knowledge worker" and how a talent marketplace may be an answer to the advancing workforce planning challenges.

In a survey the authors conducted, they found that only 27% of the respondents felt that their companies are effective at matching talent and opportunities. [2]

Our proposition is that the philosophy and process of talent acquisition should be converted in the corporate lexicon to include internal and external individuals alike. Talent, after all, is transferable and the concept of staying inside an organization or going outside shouldn't be mutually exclusive. Bryan and Joyce bring out an option; they suggest the concept of "Talent Marketplaces."

> *"We believe there is a better approach, which we call a "talent marketplace," that enables managers to "pull" talent while simultaneously giving talent a greater choice over which assignment to take. The idea is to design and build marketplaces that use market mechanisms to match the self-interest of managers looking to fill their job with the best available talent."* [3]

FIGURE 8-1
Five Program Modules

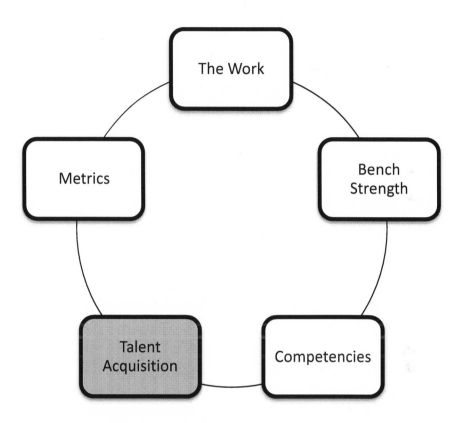

Focus on the results

When we consult with companies on their talent acquisition areas we probe on two aspects. First, we conduct an in-depth assessment which includes a web based survey and individual meetings with executives and internal customers. In our discussions we often find a consistent set of complaints describing the ineffectiveness of the talent acquisition process. The customers believe the group is not responsive to their needs, not very good at problem solving, not very creative and lack judgment and abilities to communicate or update them on the status of the projects or assignments.

Secondly, we assess the group responsible for the talent acquisition process. We discuss the same issues and they claim the hiring managers don't respond to their messages, are slow to give them updates on their needs and basically don't partner with them.

Additionally, the recruiters feel that they don't have the resources needed to do the job, are strapped with non-competitive salaries and geography which is unappealing to candidates. They feel that the positions they recruit for are routine, and unchallenging. In general, recruiters believe their internal customers have an unfairly cast negative opinion of their work. They seek to be more responsive but feel stuck as administrative persons and not as technical and functional experts.

Often, the solutions which are applied to solve these issues are to spend more dollars on technology such as instituting a highly sophisticated applicant tracking system. In our estimation, 80% of the time companies throw away monies by overly investing in technology and only 20% of the time do they invest in their recruiters.

In our consulting practices we additionally ask, can a bad model be improved by adding technology? The answer is no. Next we ask, "Can a bad model be fixed by better performing recruiting professionals?" The answer is yes.

> ➤ **What other companies are doing.**

The companies in our research believe the Workforce Planning program has a direct impact on the Talent Acquisition process. Two aspects stand out in our study:

1. The first is that over 80% of the companies we surveyed have made changes to their Talent Acquisition process as a result of what they have learned from their workforce planning process.

2. The second is evidenced by the chart below. These organizations believe their workforce planning will improve the "quality" of the hire they will make in the future. [4]

FIGURE 8-2

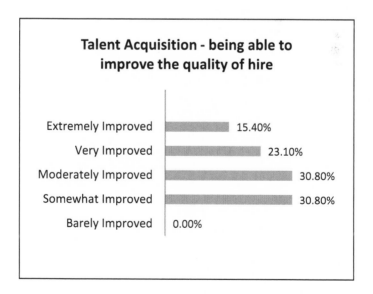

Talent Acquisition - being able to improve the quality of hire

Extremely Improved	15.40%
Very Improved	23.10%
Moderately Improved	30.80%
Somewhat Improved	30.80%
Barely Improved	0.00%

What We Have Found

In our studies and consulting practice we find many companies need to revamp and improve their talent acquisition processes and teams in order to achieve the goals and strategic human capital plans for the business to succeed. Here are several aspects of our research: 5

Brand your company's strategic uniqueness. Describe what is different and attractive about your company. On your web site and promotional materials, craft a message which emphasizes *why* candidates should be attracted to working in your company.

Develop a better ability for forecasting as you define the needs through your workforce planning across business units. As you get better at predicting and utilize more efficient forecasting tools you will enhance your ability to achieve optimum performance in your talent acquisition efforts.

The issues you will enhance and gain better control over include:
- ✓ Match the resources to the client side deliverables.
- ✓ Achieve financial profit projections by mediating the human capital investment.
- ✓ Predict and forecast demand – human capital competencies and KSAs.
- ✓ Diagnose the inventory and supply of human capital as the stable part of the organization.
- ✓ Leverage a flexible external resource to supplement the needs (fill the gaps).
- ✓ Initiate pipeline of passive candidates.
- ✓ Invest in creative methods of sourcing the best in the field.

Most organizations need to improve the proficiency of their recruiters. The areas we find they typically lack strength are:

- Communication skills
- Proactive sourcing for candidates
- Managing customers
- Teaming
- Passive recruiting
- Research
- Forecasting

One of our recommendations is to create a cross function and trans-business unit *Strategic Talent Acquisition Council.* This group would have rotating members specifically focused on advancing new tools, resources and advising on improvements in the talent acquisition process.

Improve Your Talent Acquisition Protocol

Frequently we find companies are challenged to build and maintain a "pipeline" of best prospects for their business needs. Invariably the feedback we get from hiring managers is that the talent acquisition group has to "reinvent the wheel" every time a need for a great candidate is presented. We feel your pain. In the next few pages we will present alternatives for you to consider improving your talent acquisition processes.

FIGURE 8-3

Model for a Proactive Program

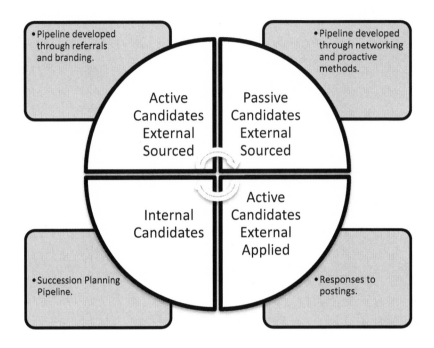

> ➢ In most organizations only 50% of the available options are being exercised.
> ➢ Capital is often spent on external recruiters/search and the issue is that they own the resume and the candidate.
> ➢ There is a need left unfilled by utilizing outsourced options besides search.
> ➢ There typically is no proactive pipeline building.
> ➢ We also recommend an assessment process customized for your company intended to select the right candidate.

FIGURE 8-4

Candidate Flow Options

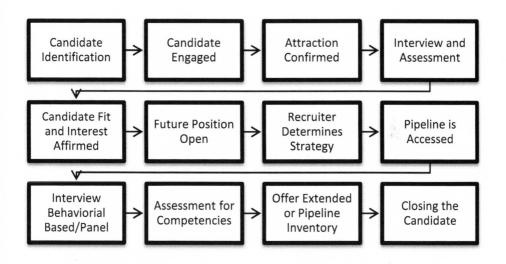

Successful Talent Acquisition Programs options:
> ➤ Proactive sourcing methodology with ongoing prospecting.
> ➤ Proficiency in candidate relationship and attraction skills.
> ➤ Proficiency in candidate referral and networking abilities.
> ➤ Assessments for identifying the correct candidate.

FIGURE 8-5

Proportions for a Sustainable
Talent Acquisition Process

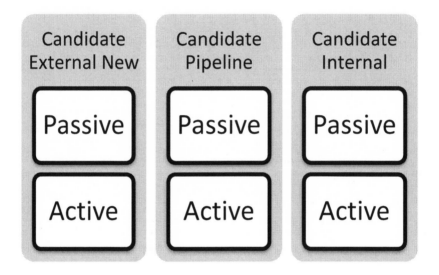

Highest level of efficiency is to have 2/3 of candidates coming from established sources both internal and pipeline. Each channel has candidates actively looking or passively interested. Both categories are options for referrals to build the inventory and pipeline. Recommendation is to expand the proficiency of the recruiter to be able to find the ideal candidate.

> ➤ **How you can use this in your company.**

The tools we have designed are examples which we know will be useful for your organization. Please follow the steps and then customize them for your own needs. They should be excellent starters but are not intended to be used for every organization in the same way.

Our Research Brings Focus

In our research, we identified specific competencies which the best performing recruiters. We also identified behaviors the high-performing recruiters and the behaviors poor performing recruiters don't have. In literature we found that researchers have determined that recruiters do impact the hiring decisions made by organizations. They do this by their purposeful behaviors focused on the identification, attraction and selection of applicants.

Our findings define how individual recruiters are more effective as a result of using different methods of proactively identifying and then attracting high-performing applicants. Proactive recruiters are more likely to attract high-performers to the company. When a recruiter is engaged in non-recruiting activities, such as administrative and coordination work, their effectiveness drops significantly.

Throughout this study we looked for areas in recruiting that the recruiter can control. In addition, there are practical and actionable events a recruiting organization can implement to maximize the effects of their recruiting efforts with the fewest possible resources. We found the number one thing that recruiting organizations can do is to train their recruiters on the competencies most impacting to recruiting activities. The training we advocate should be focused on specifics as identified in a validated instrument. An assessment can be used to identify areas critical to a recruiter's success, and the feedback and results from the assessment would then be useful in training and coaching that recruiter to improve.

In order to improve your talent acquisition processes, you need to select the recruiters with the same scrutiny used in selecting individuals for other senior professional skilled positions. Also, you should invest in professional development for this group in addition to any technology you invest in. By helping the individuals in the group grow in their professionalism and proficiency in recruiting skills, your company will become stronger and more competitive. Put the investment in people and delay the investment in technology. Investing in an outsourcing option or a new software program is not the long-term answer for the majority of companies. [6]

Checklist for your organization

The next step for your taskforce is to decipher specific needs and set an agenda for the program. The checklists can be used to refine your needs. The results will be transferrable to your *90 Day Action Plan*. Take the results from the team members and summarize in this checklist.

FIGURE 8-6

Taskforce Objectives	Summarize Needs	Next Steps
Branding		
Diversity and Inclusion		
Pipeline for Passive Candidates		
Recruiter Proficiency		
Behavioral Based Interviewing		
Competencies Utilized		

9. Metrics

If you were able to calculate in advance the efficiency of every process you wouldn't need to build in metrics. Since that is rarely the case, we delve into what it takes for a successful measurement protocol.

One noteworthy system found in high-performing organizations is how they not only believe in measuring their business operations; they also apply measuring techniques and tools to their human capital strategies. These organizations realize that appropriately designed performance measures can gauge the success of programs. By analyzing and applying metrics to human capital planning programs you are able to identify the impact and contribution these programs have in the success of the business operation as a whole.

Metrics should be an interlocking system in which data are at the service of the strategy and the strategy is responsive to the data. Asking the proper questions when designing a metric process is the first step to identifying the right areas to evaluate. Quite often companies are afraid to ask the tough questions. We will provide additional resources to solve that problem.

Metrics have to be independently <u>agreed upon as a valuable measure </u>and they have to be <u>interrelated to a business objective</u>. A metric can't meet only one criterion it must meet both.

FIGURE 9-1

Five Program Modules

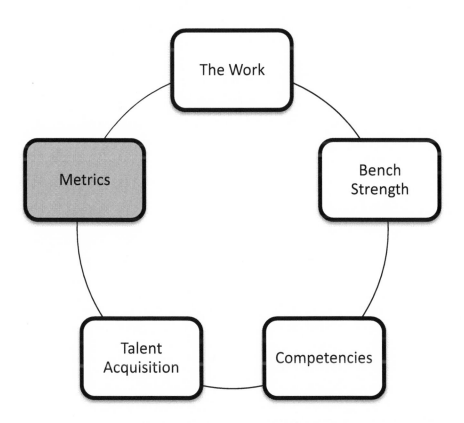

Reliable Measures Will Make the Difference

It is absolutely critical that the progress of a successful human capital program link directly to the strategies of the operation. Establishing checkpoints will allow you to make adjustments to your program.

What are your reliable measures used to determine the success or lack thereof when it comes to forecasting and selecting trend indicators for human capital? Many organizations fail to capture a clear image of human capital planning because they do not identify the proper metric in the first place. Instead, they re-cast tools and techniques borrowed from another organization or attempt to re-calibrate productivity measures ultimately selecting an inaccurate and flawed process.

A more appropriate model for reliability in human capital metrics incorporates a "loss metric" as well as a "what if" modeling simulation. These two creative aspects are necessary because they take into account a wider array of information and data necessary for prediction.

A "loss metric" means determining the amount of loss related to the gap created by filling a position in your organizational structure or leaving the vacancy open. It is a way to create a link of financial impact to the importance of the position.

A "what if" simulation means overlaying strategic scenario simulations and looking for more links to the possibility of something happening. It follows in parallel with utilizing a segmentation planning process where you are seeking to understand the individual areas impacting your program. Both of these techniques bring an advantage to measuring and forecasting.

When McKinsey&Company created a ground breaking formula called the 7-S structure, they defined seven areas to consider when looking at performance issues in an organizational structure. It subsequently has been adapted to many different models and techniques all around a holistic approach to understanding how the organization of the future needs to be evaluated. McKinsey&Company felt that there is more complexity in organizations and it is clear that if the 1970s were complex 2008 is at least equally challenging.[1]

Measuring is important. Equally important is returning to the measuring device to check on the validity of the information. In the following pages we recommend several options and various models to begin using. Take this section as a serious and equally weighted module for your program.

What are you doing intentionally?

In order to understand metrics and the role they play, it is critical to establish where you are. Many organizational issues need to be considered. Rudimentary issues faced by every organization include; how they set goals, reward achievement, define their structure in organizational charts, steps and processes to motivate and evaluate their employees. What steps are taken to audit or measure effectiveness of these processes? In the majority of cases, even these simple and necessary procedures and policies are not assessed.

So there is no misunderstanding, metrics are not dry or static numbers jotted down and tabulated. They are not anecdotes whispered in the halls and carried down to the senior leaders whose opinions weigh on the success or failure of a program. And, they are not impressions you get after attending group training sessions.

Metrics have to be:
- ✓ *Agreed upon as a valuable measure*
- ✓ *Interrelated to a business objective*

> ## What other companies are doing.

The measurement and evaluation of any process intended to improve an area of your company is absolutely critical and this program is no exception. These are all legitimate tools. Our recommendations are to make an effort at using financial measures and business unit metrics. In addition, we recommend that you implement customized metrics for this program. Do not rely on general HR metrics. The bottom line is you will need to have a legitimate, believable tool and metric process to sustain the program. [2]

FIGURE 9-2
Metric Tools Used by HR

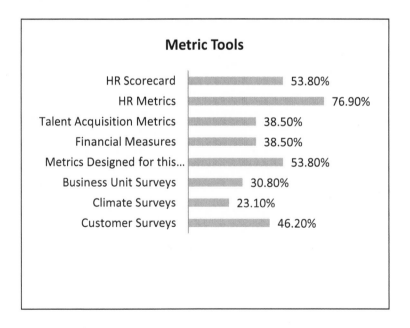

Metric Tools

HR Scorecard	53.80%
HR Metrics	76.90%
Talent Acquisition Metrics	38.50%
Financial Measures	38.50%
Metrics Designed for this...	53.80%
Business Unit Surveys	30.80%
Climate Surveys	23.10%
Customer Surveys	46.20%

Four Basic Approaches

The following approaches for analyzing the effectiveness of your workforce planning program are research-based and fundamental. These approaches are *Key Indicators, Reputational, Analytic and Strategic.* Each approach has benefits and liabilities. For the most part you can't go wrong by selecting one and moving to a custom approach or possibly a hybrid. [3]

Key Indicators Approach

The key indicators approach is the best know and most established. For workforce planning each of the identified areas in the program will have a series of indicators you will need to select. Having the taskforce, or project leaders within the business areas, participate in the ones that are most important will gain buy-in.

You will need to identify specific indicators for each module as "bell-weather" marks that are trusted to indicate a success point or a need for course correction. You will need to communicate these indicators and train the staff on methods for collecting the data.

Once collected, the results should periodically be presented to senior management. It could be to your advantage to design and use a dashboard which can be accessed through a shared hard drive and viewed by managers on a more frequent basis. By tracking upward and downward trends, the individuals responsible can be alerted when a program falls outside of the established parameters.

One advantage of this approach is the ability to identify measure and capture quantifiable information to make more data-driven decisions. By using a web-based dashboard you can take advantage of the available technology. It also allows some flexibility for changing and adapting the key measures over time.

The challenge on solely using this approach is misconstruing the data or ultimately focusing on the symptoms and not addressing the root cause of a problem. Also, using a selected approach of only a few data points may bring dissension if a group feels the indicator is out of their control to impact it. On the reverse side, if managers do control the input they may corrupt the data and skew the results in their favor.

Reputational Approach

This approach focuses on the perceived value or contributions the workforce planning program is affecting. It is a reflection of the stakeholders view.

In this approach you will seek to identify the most important customers of the workforce planning program and then design and administer (or acquire) a survey to determine customer satisfaction data concerning the services provided. As you collect, analyze and summarize data showing results in graphical impact, you will then use the information generated to improve the quality and delivery system of the program.

This process brings into sharp focus the service mission of the workforce planning program and targets the extent to which line managers are receiving the high-quality HR advice, program, service, solutions and support they expect.

We caution you when using this approach. Be careful to not misinterpret the qualitative side of this data and draw conclusions of success because the "feelings" are that the program is effective.

Analytic Approach

This approach is comprised of a number of techniques attempting to determine the net value or benefit of the program. It is most often expressed in monetary or nonmonetary terms.

In this approach you will be looking for more science to validate the programs. You will need to identify the outcome measure to be used for evaluating the program and look to statistically examine the extent to which the program had a positive impact on the desired outcome measure.

The advantages in considering an analytic approach is that it shows the company the benefits of workforce planning impact and in many cases financial results can be calculated. In addition, it brings attention to specific programs that should be added or dropped as well as being supported by the business units because it "speaks their language" in terms of return on an investment.

The down side of pure analytics is that they may cause a narrowing of the focus eliminating programs with mostly intangibles.

Strategic Approach

As HR seeks to become more strategic, this approach is instrumental. Instead of focusing on the pure measurement approach, this technique is one which mirrors the workforce planning goals with the strategy of the business. It is solely focused on supporting the business strategy.

Identify the firm's overall strategy (as determined by top leaders) and confirm that the workforce planning program matches the structure and outline of the business unit. Outline the HR and workforce planning policies and procedures that would best assist the firm to achieve its strategic objectives.

Be prepared for an uphill battle to implement a strategic approach if your organization is highly complex with multiple business units and different organizational structures. Also, bringing change to these environments often involves customizing the process raising the degree of difficulty.[4]

Steps for your taskforce...

This is an exercise for your taskforce, leaders, or HR team. It also is a critical component for addressing the current inventory of skills and competencies in your company.

Select a model to begin basing your approach for measuring. Create your own or use different aspects of these and make a hybrid.

_____

_____

_____

_____

_____

_____

_____

_____

> ## How you can use this in your company.

The metrics we will use to monitor the implementation include the following... Check all that apply.

FIGURE 9-3

Key Area	Apply
Ensure line manager's buy-in.	
Design a process to overcome any organizational structure issues.	
Secure senior leadership support and a budget to support to the program.	
Design a model which will transfer across business units and countries.	
Select or design a technology platform for analyzing data.	
Research and benchmark workforce planning: ✓ *Attend conferences or workshops* ✓ *Purchase books, materials* ✓ *Conduct benchmarking* ✓ *Form an exploratory taskforce* ✓ *Hire consultants* ✓ *Conduct in-depth research* ✓ *We recommend going an additional step and have a certified master trainer in workforce planning.*	
Determine the timeline and pilot group.	

> ➤ **How you can use this in your company.**

The metrics we will use to determine the effectiveness of our workforce planning program include ways to measure our ability to respond to these global trends... Check all that apply.

FIGURE 9-4

Global Trends	Apply
Tightening Labor Market	
Industry Consolidations	
Availability of Technology	
Competition for Technical/Managerial Talent	
Emerging Markets	
Larger and More Complex Organizations	
Competition for Talent Will Intensify	
Shifting Organizational Structures	
Aging Population in the Labor Market	
Retirement of Workers in Our Company	
Availability of Skilled Workers	
Global Talent Challenges	
Tightening Labor Market	

> ## How you can use this in your company.

The metrics we will use to determine the effectiveness of our workforce planning program include... Check all that apply. FIGURE 9-5

Key Measure	Apply
Create a dashboard for business leaders to track ongoing progress.	
Seek to have them emphasized in the company's annual report.	
Will be constructed with input from the business units.	
Will be presented to the senior leadership team annually.	
Will be periodically audited.	
Quality of hires.	
Voluntary turnover rates.	
Changes in assessment scores (360 – multi-rater).	
Changes in performance management Ranking scores.	
Changes in industry percentile ranking.	
Diversity/inclusion tracking.	
Improvement or decline in talent acquisition costs.	
Improvement in training.	
Customer service survey scores.	
Improvement in overall turnover rates.	
Evaluate effectiveness of recruiting methods.	
Evaluating the performance improvement in business units based on a predetermined key indicator measure.	

Checklist for your organization

The next step for your taskforce is to decipher specific needs and set an agenda for the program. The results will be transferrable to your *90 Day Action Plan*.

FIGURE 9-6

Taskforce Objectives	Summarize Needs	Next Steps
Ideal Organization		
Five Sections for Leaders		
KSAs for Future		
Communication Tools		
Cautions		
Key Position		
Strategic Segmentation		
Principles Applied		

Research is the hallmark of our data-driven approach. The 90 Day Action Plan will be the road map for your competitive future.

Part VI

Designing
Your 90 Day
Action Plan

10. Incremental Steps

This book is the new paradigm for human capital planning. Challenges exist with every worthwhile venture. Make proactive decisions and don't let the challenges persist. Recruit champions; look for believers who insist the company rise above the competition.

The doctor's advice, "take baby steps." That was the prescription Dr. Leo Marvin gave to his patient the classic text book case neurotic Bob Wiley. Bob and Leo are leading characters in the cinematic comedy titled *What About Bob?* Dr. Marvin (Richard Dreyfuss) a successful psychiatrist had just written a self-help book titled *Baby Steps* and was using the formula to treat the self-diagnosed highly obsessive-compulsive Bob Wiley (Bill Murray.) The principles in the imaginary *Baby Steps* are to take small actions in a positive direction and only focus on one step at a time. Don't get overwhelmed by the big picture. Take a hint from the recommendations that Dr. Leo Marvin gave to Bob Wiley. As you begin to make changes in your life or in this case in your organization, "take baby steps."

Unless you have seen the movie *What About Bob?,* or you are an aficionado of movies with Bill Murray, this reference might not be familiar to you. The advice is still sound. Any large scale implementation is fraught with pitfalls and resistance. By taking small incremental movements you will avoid tripping into a problem and have the time to garner the support you need.[1]

Our intention in writing this **Handbook** is to bring you the combination of high-level strategic insights, research-based tactics, and a toolkit to begin your customized implementation. In the next 90 days, when you follow the steps we outline, you will gain the knowledge and abilities to structure the concepts and sow the seeds. Our belief is that with a process centered on 90 day increments you will be able to define realistic and actionable framework to craft a successful agenda for a more strategic direction in your human capital planning.

Set your goals with incremental milestones yet make them grand enough to attract the inertia to overcome the obstacles you will face.

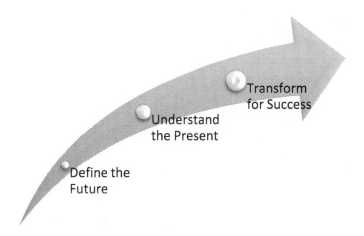

FIGURE 10-1

Five Program Modules

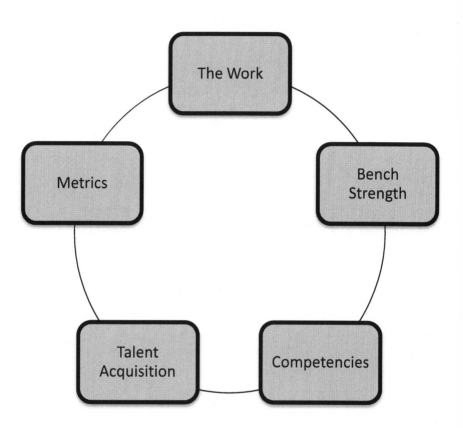

Caution: Do not begin a program with half a heart because it will be doomed to fail. By starting with a partial commitment, your taskforce members may become easily dissuaded at the first sign of conflict or disagreement. Success will come only with a fully focused commitment and resolve to impact the company for the good of all.

Co-creation Improves Program Design

In the initial phase of designing your workforce planning program setting a process of co-creation not only will advance the program development but it will ensure a higher level of buy-in.   Co-creation is the act of having multiple resources developing the *same product* in the *same time frame.*

As the taskforce begins to execute the list of objectives in these early days we recommend you investigate the help of outside experts and resources.   By having two groups designing the same components in parallel you will gain insights that help shape a stronger program.

The *open-system* approach will allow you to consider multiple points of view and access to the development process.   When you leverage other intellects, the innovation will enhance the effectiveness of your program. The goal is to innovate early using a series of check points in close proximity.

For instance, have the team members coordinate their product development by meeting twice weekly to de-brief and determine what the next step will be.   These early meetings will accelerate the design process. Allow each member and co-creator to editorialize on the overall development. Giving open and free-range comment will drive a more critical process because there will be no holding back because of hidden political agendas. The goal is to develop sound fundamentals to build the framework for the next stage.

The initial stage and most important part of the program wraps around the need to gain agreement on the design and the metrics. This opening section will be for the project team to develop and design the protocol and process flow, program criteria, and make use of the metrics to evaluate the program as defined by the business needs.

In the chapters following; *The First 30 Days, The Next 30 Days, and The Last 30 Days,* we outline what your "baby steps" are. The methods you use may vary based on your company and your need. This process focuses on compiling the information from your taskforce members into a single resource.

In order to have a successful kick-off we recommend using a workshop to introduce each section and module. By following an iterative design format you can focus on defining a workforce planning program, understanding the elements, and learning the needed components to ensure a successful implementation.

11. The First 30 Days

Keep the Faith

For many organizations, committing to a workforce planning program will require a leap of faith. There will be numerous times that the negative voices in your organization will lobby for only doing a half or partial approach because you are suggesting too much change. Keep in mind, every organization is made up of individuals seeking to hold on to the past, creating pockets of managers who are "unconvinced" that improvement is needed or that it will work. Don't be discouraged. By following the negative voices your process will be diluted. Let them sit on the side line; that is their prerogative. We want to express our encouragement to "keep the faith" and push forward.

Process Overview

Our implementation process is a multipronged approach. As you begin the first 30 days there are cautions to plan for that we will re-emphasize.

- ✓ **Secure senior leaders as champions.** In order to achieve the senior leadership buy-in you need, plan to build a comprehensive business case on the state of your workforce and why this process will be a solution.

- ✓ **Make sure you have a budget established.** This is the most difficult challenge to overcome. If there is too little commitment from senior leaders and they do not designate a budget for this program it is doubtful it will succeed.

- ✓ **Your taskforce should draft a charter and include a communication and marketing platform to educate the line managers and gain their buy-in.** In our research, over 60% of the participants indicated the biggest challenge was overcoming the hesitancy of the line managers to participate. They failed to see the long-term benefits and did not express support. Given that the business units are the major players in this program it is important to get them on-board early in the process.

- ✓ **Determine who will lead your initiative.** Our research shows that there is a need for a dedicated individual to lead the team of business unit representatives.

✓ **Establish your reasons for a workforce planning program and build your business case.**

✓ **Plan and communicate your agendas, meeting protocol and deliverables.**

✓ **Coordinate the implementation schedule and confirm all steps are communicated to the senior leadership.**

✓ **This first 30 days you will spend doing all the upfront leg work, benchmarking, and establishing the necessary tools.**

✓ **Each taskforce member should have a copy of this book.** We recommend going an additional step of getting individuals certified as master trainers in workforce planning.

✓ **Read and digest the Overview, Part I Making the Business Case and Part II Creating the Road Map in the book to help set your calendar and agenda.**

✓ **Research and benchmark workforce planning:**
  o *Attend conferences or workshops*
  o *Purchase books, materials*
  o *Conduct benchmarking*

Transfer the data and information generated by the taskforce. For this section complete the following exercises.

Page Number	Completed?
Page 12	
Pages 33-35	
Page 66-67	
Pages 81	
Page 91	

In this segment you will want to consider using the following tools we have designed for you. They are found in the Appendix.

Tools #	Title
001	Seven Step Methodology
002	Overview of the Process (Future)
005	Data Points
006	Defining the Workforce Needs

12. The Next 30 Days

The Seeds, Roots, Branches and Fruit

Wide sweeping innovation and organizational change will require you to cultivate the ground and sow the seeds to prepare your company to move in a direction for which it has no precedent.

In building this framework look for internal "customer insights" by testing and seeking opinions and understanding the needs of the stakeholders. These insights should influence the design of your workforce planning program in a positive and proactive way. When you extract the value from these interactions the ad hoc collaboration from these customers will improve the design and implementation process. Consider taking a customer survey and tap into focus groups early. These data points will give you added support early on as well as indicate areas needing improvement.

By eliciting the requirements of the stakeholders early-on you will be able to understand the relationship between transformational and transactional elements.

By understanding the difference between the two in these early stages of development you will dramatically improve chances for success.

You will need to prepare to overcome the orthodox management principles and decision making which have rooted your company in its current state of reactive v. proactive approaches. There no doubt will be painful times and eventual restructurings. All are the price to be paid for securing the human capital destined to lead your company into the future.

As you proceed, the workforce planning strategy becomes a master blue print to design and build a company *on purpose*. It will be tied to major fundamentals to get the organization to work differently. We are talking about a living organism. In the same way you would till a field or prune an orchard, so too will this course of action identify the HR programs producing fruit and the ones needing improvement. In the next 30 day time frame our program calls for you to establish metrics, competencies and select the technology you will use to mine and store data.

Process Overview

✓ **Define the critical roles and functions.** Once you begin to determine the pilot area and the business unit where you will begin the use this process start at the top with "Key Positions" identified and competencies crafted.

✓ **Analyze your organizational structure and plan on efforts to ensure collaboration**. If there is little cooperation or communication between your business units, then this program will be difficult to use. It is critical to have an understanding and collaboration to tie specifics to the talent acquisition and talent development needs for each business unit.

✓ **Train the HR leaders, Senior Leaders and Business Unit Leaders.** Schedule your team training or achieving for workforce planning and develop the tools and techniques you will need.

✓ **Select your pilot group and focus the first part of the implementation.** In order to attain early success, seek pilot areas which will make an impact you can use as evidence and refine the program prior to rolling it out enterprise wide.

✓ **Design metrics for evaluating the performance improvement in business units based on a predetermined key indicator measures.**

✓ **Design a model which will transfer across business units and countries.**

✓ **Select or design a technology platform for analyzing data.**

✓ **Metrics you will want to consider:**
   o Quality of hires.
   o Voluntary turnover rates.
   o Changes in assessment scores (360 – multi-rater).
   o Changes in performance management ranking and scores.
   o Changes in industry percentile ranking.
   o Diversity/inclusion tracking.
   o Improvement or decline in talent acquisition costs.
   o Improvement in training.
   o Evaluate effectiveness of recruiting methods.

✓ **Create a dashboard for business leaders to track ongoing progress.**
   o Design with input from the business units.
   o Presented to the senior leadership team annually.

✓ **Design a competency model**
   o Utilize tools for defining, validating, tie to business strategy.
   o Format a protocol for documenting and tying to performance.

Transfer the data and information
generated by the taskforce. For this
section complete the following
exercises.

Page Number	Completed?
Page 105	
Page 115	
Page 119	
Page 123	
Page 127	
Pages 138-141	

In this segment you will want to consider
using the following tools we have designed for
you. They are found in the Appendix.

Tools #	Title
001	Seven Step Methodology
003	Overview of the Process (Current)
004	Replacement Policy
005	Data Points
006	Defining the Workforce Needs
007	Strategic Communication Tools Level I
008	Strategic Communication Tools Level II
009	Strategic Communication Tools Level III
010	Strategic Communication Tools Level IV
011	Competency Modeling Phase I
012	Competency Modeling Phase II

13. The Last 30 Days

Unbundle the Modules

Now is the point of converting the final ingredients of your workforce planning recipe into a usable intervention. You may not have every module complete but we are confident you will have made sufficient progress to recognize the next step(s) needing attention.

Unbundle the modules and identify the next high-value target. You may be ready to kick-off your pilot. Or you may have decided to build or refine your competency model. Our modular design encourages you to set open-minded criteria that are achievable. In increments of 30 days at a time targeting a 90 day outcome your co-creators and internal taskforce members should have an overview prepared to update senior management.

As you wrap up the first 90 days of your action plan try to leverage the tools we have provided, research best practices, benchmark with the best, seek out emerging trends from a wide array of industries and look for opportunities to catalyze change so you can shape your organization to be more competitive.

Process Overview

This process overview is a catchall and it is up to you to begin to unbundle the program as you see fit.

- ✓ **Continue to define the critical roles and functions.**

- ✓ **Continue to analyze your organizational structure and plan on efforts to ensure collaboration.**

- ✓ **Complete any unfinished training for the HR leaders, Senior Leaders and Business Unit Leaders.**

- ✓ **Implement the pilot program.**

- ✓ **Design a model which will transfer across business units and countries.**

- ✓ **Select or design a technology platform for analyzing data.**

- ✓ **Finalize the metrics and process you will use.**

- ✓ **Create a dashboard for business leaders to track ongoing progress.**
  - o Design with input from the business units.
  - o Present to the senior leadership team annually.

- ✓ **Finalize the competency model**
  - o Validate the competencies.
  - o Format a protocol for documenting and tying to performance.

Transfer the data and information generated by the taskforce. For this section complete the following exercises.

Page Number	Completed?
Page 155	
Pages 165-169	

In this segment you will want to consider using all of the tools we have designed for you. They are found in the Appendix.

Tools #	Title
001	Seven Step Methodology
002	Overview of the Process (Future)
003	Overview of the Process (Current)
004	Replacement Policy
005	Data Points
006	Defining the Workforce Needs
007	Strategic Communication Tools Level I
008	Strategic Communication Tools Level II
009	Strategic Communication Tools Level III
010	Strategic Communication Tools Level IV
011	Competency Modeling Phase I
012	Competency Modeling Phase II
013	Performance Management
014	Supply of Current KSAs
015	Geographic Indicators
016	Talent Acquisition Quarterly Objectives
017	Talent Development Quarterly Objectives

Don't Stop Here

Now is the time to plan and set in motion the next phase of your program. You have dedicated the resources necessary to craft a customized foundation for your human capital plan. Our recommendation is that you focus on the successes of your pilot group. Determine the areas that need improvement and select the business unit you will put in your next phase. In addition, by following the same format in our program you should be able to report the successes of the process to senior leadership.

Break down the pieces and take our suggestions on using a modular program. The taskforce should be meeting weekly at this point and anticipating a timeline for the next three quarters which means you will have a process stretching over one full year. That is the key. Take our *90 Day Action Plan* and create an enterprise-wide program. It ultimately will make your company more competitive and flexible than ever thought possible.

For the next 90 days of your workforce planning program create a formula that takes your company closer to the goal. As the legendary coach of the National Football League Kansas City Chiefs Hank Stram put so succinctly when he encouraged his players, "Just keep matriculating the ball down the field boys."

14.Closing Argument

There is no downside! A comprehensive workforce planning program only represents upside potential for your organization and employees. Still not convinced?

Let's look at it from a different angle. In a trial, the opposing counsels begin by making opening statements. They outline their view of the case and how they will attempt to persuade the jury their argument is correct. After they present their evidence and interview the witnesses, both sides deliver a "closing argument." Each attorney is trying to re-emphasize the validity and strength of their argument as they attempt to persuade the judge and jury to rule in their favor.

Just as the attorneys present their closing arguments, we will share again our research-based insights and the favorable impact a workforce planning program will have on your organization.

The Definition

Strategic workforce planning is the alignment of human capital with the diagnosed business needs. It is a comprehensive approach to delivering HR processes, and when properly executed, each business entity will have the right person in the right job at the right time. Workforce planning programs have to deliver on these points.

- ✓ These skills and competencies relate to the defined work as understood in present existence and the future need.

- ✓ The designated needs are juxtaposed against an existing inventory revealing gaps.

- ✓ These gaps are subsequently planned to be addressed through external acquisition, professional development, or succession planning.

- ✓ The success of the program is determined by the same standard of excellence any business venture is measured.

- ✓ It has to make the company more profitable.

The Research

In July and August 2008 we conducted a seminal benchmark study on workforce planning. We surveyed HR professionals and asked them to tell us how satisfied they were with their ability to match-up the human capital with the business unit needs over the next five years. This was regardless if they had a workforce planning program or not. The results from our research reveals that nearly three quarters of the HR leaders interviewed felt they could meet the strategic human capital needs of their respective business units less than half of the time. [1]

Effective workforce planning requires a strongly collaborative effort. Our research pinpointed challenges companies faced in implementing and sustaining workforce planning programs. One barrier to an effective workforce planning program is a company that has an organizational structure with the business units in silos where each one is independent and self reliant. [2]

A shining illustration of a company that has broken down these walls, shifted from a silo structured organization, and is an evolving experiment in collaboration is Cisco. The San Jose, California based technology giant has created a radical new organizational mandate. The company now emphasizes 70% of their decision making comes from teams, councils and collaborative efforts among business units which previously had competed against each other for resources. These changes have, so far, been wildly successful. By rewarding and encouraging collaboration, Cisco saw "a tenfold increase in new projects," according to Vice President Ron Ricci. He also reflected that operating expenses have been trimmed and they are increasing their profits. [3]

Workforce planning is strategically not only significant for you and your company's future; it is the one tool the HR leaders can take to their business unit executives with confidence that it will improve the competitive capabilities of the organization as a whole.

The Evidence

The population that is 55 and older will increase much more sharply between 1995 and 2025; more so than any other age group. Overall, the Census Bureau projects that the aging trend in the nation will be affected by the baby boom generation until 2040. [4]

The labor pool is shrinking but not just shrinking as a result of retirement. It is far more complicated and it is cause for concern. At the same time, the debate rages over the potential shortfall in labor and skills. Further complications are occurring as the aging workers possessing critical knowledge they are replaced by not only a younger group but one which will be put in charge with often little time to prepare.

Our organization conducted an international webcast on workforce planning in February 2008 with 509 different individuals registering representing 33 different countries. We conducted a pulse-poll and asked how many of the participants were actively engaged in a workforce planning program. We found that 68% of the participants had no workforce planning strategy what so ever. [5]

The Program

This program is designed for modular implementation. We have taken the guess work out of what you need and provided the tools for you get started. In most cases, there is some part of this process already in your company. Our recommendation is to start from the beginning. Understand the trends affecting your company and establish a baseline. Next you can move into envisioning the future and move on from there. Our modular process makes this both affordable and realistic.

30-60-90 Day Action Plan

We understand you may have difficulty grasping the concept of the *90 Day Action Plan*. It may not seem possible. You are asking how all the pieces can fit in this puzzle in one fourth of a year. Think about it:

* ❖ By reading this book we have outlined the tasks, techniques, and tools to "get started."
* ❖ By setting incremental tasks and goals in 30 day time frames you are able to get the program lined up and started. It is realistic.
* ❖ By continuing to deliver additional new modules over the 90 days you will keep the executives and internal clients motivated.

This process is iterative, it changes and grows as you customize and learn what your company needs. Once you have completed the first 90 days go on to the next 90 days and before you know it you will have spent a year establishing a strong planning process and are ready for integrating strategic planning into the business.

The closing argument is complete. In a trial, the case goes to the judge and jury for deliberation and consultation as they contemplate and decide the verdict. You are the judge and jury.

The decision is now in your hands.
What will it be?

Appendix

Tools

You will be on the design side as you begin to craft the structural elements of your workforce planning initiative. Design, structure, systems, and architectural integrity are nomenclature defining the orderly flow of a series of activities culminating in a new product. These terms aptly fit the world of workforce planning.

The roles you and your taskforce will play are closer to research marketers than to human resource specialists. Workforce planning requires more creative and innovative tactics than you may have had to use in the past. You will need to be part counselor, part psychologist and part statistician. This undertaking requires the use of tools which will aid you in drawing out the necessary strategic needs of your business partners. We have provided not only a set of tools but an entire blueprint. Take the guidance we provide in each module and chapter and begin to design the future for your workforce.

Seven Step Methodology
Tools 001

One of the techniques we developed for use in our workshops is called our Seven Step Methodology. It is useful especially as you engage other business partners. It also is a good tool for helping the members of your taskforce to stay focused on improving the process.

Follow the steps below for each new section you are tackling.

1. Present a scenario or series of questions which lead to identifying a need.
2. Next, set a realistic goal to answer the proposed scenario.
3. Determine a focus plan to respond to the need determined.
4. Execute going toward an objective which has been written down.
5. Review your activity in a given time frame.
6. Answer the original question based on behavior, accomplishments and learned insights.
7. Now, ask a new series of questions which lead you to a higher level.

The goal is to start with a relatively low to medium level impact question and over a series of the 7 steps move the question up and higher in impact.

Overview of the Process (Future)
Tools 002

This list provides suggestions for brainstorming and focus group conversations. The future of the company needs to be defined and positions designed. Go through it and use as you see the need. It is a great tool for guiding your taskforce.

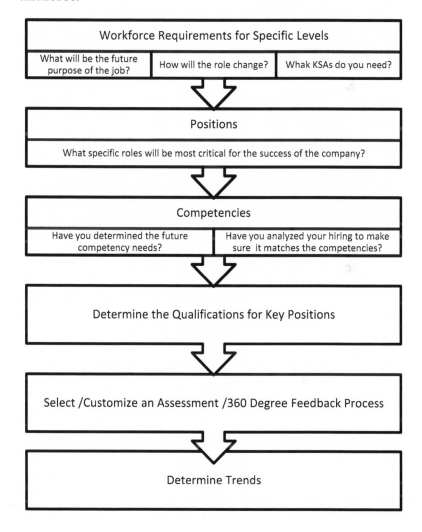

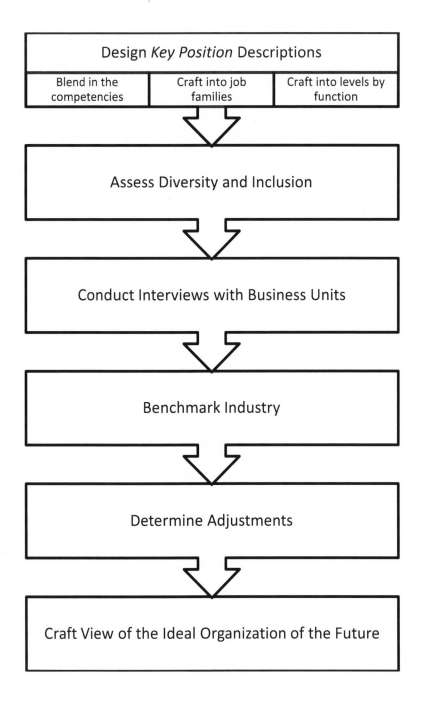

Overview of the Process (Current)
Tools 003

This list provides suggestions for brainstorming and focusing group conversations. The current view of the company needs to be defined and positions designed. It is a great tool for guiding your taskforce.

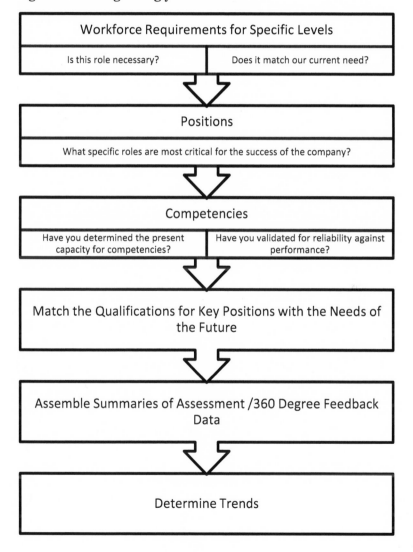

Workforce Requirements for Specific Levels

| Is this role necessary? | Does it match our current need? |

Positions

What specific roles are most critical for the success of the company?

Competencies

| Have you determined the present capacity for competencies? | Have you validated for reliability against performance? |

Match the Qualifications for Key Positions with the Needs of the Future

Assemble Summaries of Assessment /360 Degree Feedback Data

Determine Trends

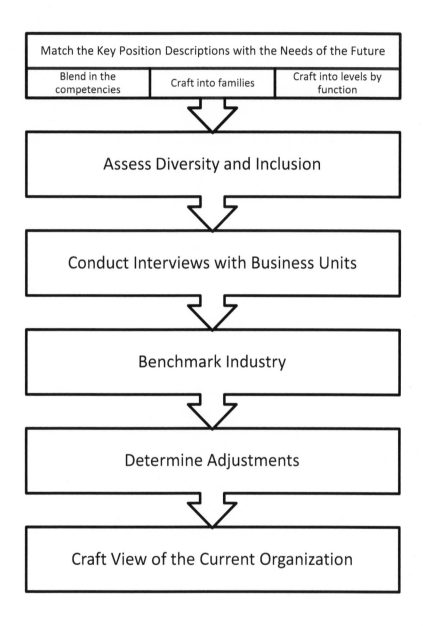

Replacement Policy
Tools 004

The first requirement is that the "key position" criteria have been determined and this role fulfills at least 80% of the criteria.

The individual has left the company voluntarily and this is not considered part of a re-organization.

The Replacement Program Model outline follows a series of questions:

> Is the position located in a primary business unit?
>> a. If *no* then leave the position open for 90 days to determine the need to replace.
>> b. If *yes* then go to the next step.

> Is there a developed pipeline from which a clear candidate slate is identified?
>> a. If *yes* then proceed to following your selection process.
>> b. If *no* then proceed to the next step.

> Is the position a leadership role responsible for four or more subordinates?
>> a. If *no* and only one to three individuals are impacted then re-distribute these individuals into a supporting structure that fits the need.
>> b. If *yes* then move to the next step.

> Can this group be considered strong enough to become a team?
>> a. If *yes* then initiate team training.
>> b. If *no* then move to the next step.

> Can the entire area be absorbed into another business group?

       a. If *yes* then begin the interview and selection process to fit and re-align.

       b. If *no* then move to the next step.

➤ Has this business been re-organized in the last 12 months?

       a. If *yes*, can the business area return to the previous structure and maintain productivity?

       b. If *yes* re-align the business and communicate the changes.

       c. If *no* then go to the next step.

➤ Initiate the steps required to seek an individual from outside the organization.

Data Points
Tools 005

Below we have provided suggestions on where you can begin to look for information and sources of data to bring more richness to your process. By analyzing the trends of your last several years you may be able to see where you will be headed. The results may not be conclusive but they may reflect what has been important in the recent past.

Conduct a comprehensive review of existing position descriptions.

1. Are they up to date (written in the last 24 months)?
2. Do they incorporate your company's competencies?
3. Has the language been updated?
4. Are they legal?

Analyze the recruiting activity you have conducted for the last three years.

1. What positions did you recruit for most?
2. How many open positions were because of attrition?
3. What business units had the most change?

What companies have you sold or bought in the past three years?

1. How have the positions in your organization been affected?
2. Did you gain individuals with skills you didn't have?
3. Did you lose individuals you considered critical?
4. What do these positions look like when you describe the skills gained and lost?

Analyze the promotions over the last three years

1. What business units?
2. What levels?
3. What skills?
4. Were competencies considered?
5. Are there gaps?
6. What role did the corporate university play in upgrading skills?

What trends do you see in the levels and skills needed in these instances?

When was the last formal job analysis completed?

1. Was it for an individual or for a level?
2. Were the results documented and tracked?
3. How were they validated?

When was the last re-organization?

1. What was the outcome in specific functions and skills?
2. Were competencies considered?
3. Were assessments (360 degree) used in evaluating the individuals?
4. What was the organization structure change if any?
5. Did the new structure stay or was it changed again in less than three years?
6. What trends do you see from this event?
7. How was the change documented?
8. What were the key learning's and how were they captured?

Defining the Workforce Needs
Tools 006

These exercises are used as you guide the business leaders to envision what they need for the future as well as a template for HR to inventory the current levels of employee skills and competency ranges.

Execution Section I					
KSA for Future	**Low**	**Low to Moderate**	**Moderate**	**Moderate to High**	**High**
Analytical Thinking					
Decision Making					
Financial Management					
Resource Management					
Continuous Improvement					
Creativity					
Collaboration					
Strategic Section II					
KSA for Future	**Low**	**Low to Moderate**	**Moderate**	**Moderate to High**	**High**
Strategic and global mindset.					
Translate a vision for the future of a work group.					
Building Partnerships					
Strategic Analysis					

Appendix

Interpersonal Section III					
KSA for Future	**Low**	**Low to Moderate**	**Moderate**	**Moderate to High**	**High**
Accountability					
Adaptability					
Resilience					
Communication					
Stress Tolerance					
Valuing Diversity					
Leadership Section IV					
KSA for Future	**Low**	**Low to Moderate**	**Moderate**	**Moderate to High**	**High**
Initiative					
Integrity					
Judgment					
Implement Plans					
Managing Conflict					
Consult/Advise					
Developing Talent					
Technical Section V					
KSA for Future	**Low**	**Low to Moderate**	**Moderate**	**Moderate to High**	**High**
Technical Solution Development					
Technology Management					

KSAs /Competency	Prepared / Not Prepared
Section I	
Section II	
Section III	
Section IV	
Section V	
Overall Areas for Focus	

Strategic Communication – Level I
Tools 007

As you process this information and begin to set up your internal meetings with your business unit partners you will need a series of guided discussion tools. This format is one to use.

Prior to meeting with your business unit partners send them this process. This first matrix is for the **Level I or Implementers.**

What roles are critical to driving the long-term strategic advantage for your business?

Describe your needs:

What impact will they have on the top-line growth?

Describe your needs:

What impact will they have on our overall company strategic direction?

Describe your needs:

Action Plan:

How will these roles give our company a competitive advantage over the competition?

Describe your needs:

Action Plan:

When it comes to calculating the fulfilling of these roles will it be to our advantage to seek to acquire these individuals or to train someone in the company?

Describe your needs:

Action Plan:

Strategic Communication –Level II
Tools 008

Prior to meeting with your business unit partners send them this process. This matrix is for the **Level II or Sustainers**. You will use the same format for each of the other three areas in the levels of needs.

What roles are critical to driving the long-term strategic advantage for your business?

Describe your needs:

What impact will they have on the top-line growth?

Describe your needs:

What impact will they have on our overall company strategic direction?

Describe your needs:

Action Plan:

How will these roles give our company a competitive advantage?

Describe your needs:

Action Plan:

When it comes to calculating the fulfillment of these roles will it be to our advantage to seek to acquire these individuals or to train someone in the company?

Describe your needs:

Action Plan:

Strategic Communication – Level III
Tools 009

Prior to meeting with your business unit partners send them this process. This matrix is for the **Level III or Essentials.** You will use the same format for each of the other three areas in the levels of needs.

What roles are critical to driving the long-term strategic advantage for our company?

Action Plan:

What impact will they have on the top-line growth?

Action Plan:

What impact will they have on our ability to achieve our strategic direction?

Action Plan:

How will these roles give our company a competitive advantage over the competition?

Action Plan:

When it comes to calculating the fulfilling of these roles will it be to our advantage to seek to acquire these individuals or to train someone in the company?

Action Plan:

Strategic Communication - Level IV
Tools 010

Prior to meeting with your business unit partners send them this process. This matrix is for the **Level IV** the **Flexible Workforce**.

What roles will be considered flexible, contract, or temporary for successfully achieving our strategic objectives?

Action Plan:

How will these roles give our company a competitive advantage over the competition?

Action Plan:

Competency Modeling Phase I
Tools 011

What was the source and method used for crafting the competencies?

Action Plan:

Confirm there is a consistency in the type of competency developed.

Action Plan:

What were the processes used in developing them?

Action Plan:

Are they linked to the business goals? How do they match the future needs?

Action Plan:

Competency Modeling Phase II
Tools 012

Was there a process for revising and confirming content?

Action Plan:

Determine the process we need to rank each competency or category for importance.

Action Plan:

Next we need to assess each category or items to determine the reliability of how the competency predicts performance.

Action Plan:

Establish a protocol for documenting the process and tracking changes.

Action Plan:

Performance Management
Tools 013

Go through each of the following areas. Complete each as needed. Capture the critical competencies and information which shows you the best view of current KSAs.

Have you determined performance standards?

Action Plan:

How attainable and realistic are those standards?

Action Plan:

What value do these performance standards deliver to the organization?

Action Plan:

When was the last time your organization completed an audit and update on position descriptions?

Action Plan:

Which business units currently have the best performers based on ROI?

Action Plan:

Supply of Current KSAs
Tools 014

Capture the critical competencies and information which shows you the best view of current KSAs.

Which business units by function have the highest level of turnover? Why?

Action Plan:

How many new positions have you created in the last three years?

Action Plan:

When you consider your recruiting efforts are they effective? How can they be improved?

Action Plan:

Who determines the KSAs which are part of each position?

Action Plan:

Are your KSAs linked directly to the performance evaluation?

Action Plan:

How would you gauge your KSAs against the competition?

Action Plan:

Geographic Indicators
Tools 015

Does your organization plan for advancing into new geographical areas?

What impact will geography have on contributing to our competitive advantage?

Action Plan:

What constraints will geography have on successfully accomplishing our strategic objectives?

Action Plan:

What challenges does our organization face as we prepare to expand into new geographic regions?

What additional resources should be considered?

Action Plan:

Talent Acquisition
Tools 016

This matrix can be used to evaluate the progressive effectiveness of the Talent Acquisition group. It is formatted to match the Strategic Segmentation levels for your workforce planning process.

Level I - What are the number of open positions?
Level II – What are the number of open positions?
Level III – What are the number of open positions?

Integrating your Talent Acquisition group into the planning process is important. This checklist can be considered a metric you may want to use. The arrows indicate the trend of the deliverables. These are examples.

Talent Acquisition Deliverables	Objective	Results 1st Qtr	Results 2nd Qtr	Results 3rd Qtr	Results 4th Qtr	Trend
Level I Pipeline	40 Open	Met Goals	Met Goals	Exceed Goals	Met Goals	→
Level II Pipeline	30 Open	Missed Target	Missed Target	Met Goals	Met Goals	←
Level III Pipeline	60 Open	Met Goals	Exceed Goals			→

Talent Development
Tools 017

This matrix can be used to evaluate the progressive effectiveness of the Talent Development group. It is formatted to match the Strategic Segmentation levels for your workforce planning process.

Level I - KSAs to be developed.
Level II – KSAs to be developed.
Level III – KSAs to be developed.

Integrating your Talent Development group into the planning process is important. This checklist can be considered a metric you may want to use. The arrows indicate the trend of the deliverables. These are examples.

Talent Development Deliverables	Objective	Results 1st Qtr	Results 2nd Qtr	Results 3rd Qtr	Results 4th Qtr	Trend
Level I individual skills and action program in place.	55 Train	Met Goals	Met Goals	Exceed Goals	Met Goals	⇨
Level II individual skills and action program in place.	25 Train	Met Goals	Met Goals	Exceed Goals	Met Goals	⇨
Level III individual skills and action program in place.	60 Train	Missed Target	Missed Target			⇦

Notes

Preface

1. "Human Capital, Key Principles for Effective Strategic Workforce Planning," United States General Accounting Office, Report to Congress, 2003.
2. Gross, Jeffrey H. 2008. *Workforce Planning Benchmark Study*, TopGrade Workforce Planning, Hudson, Ohio.
3. Young, Mary. 2006. *Strategic Workforce Planning,* Working Group Research Report, [The] Conference Board.

Introduction

1. Geerlings, Wilfred., and Kees van Veen. "The future qualities of workforces: a simulation study of the long-term consequences of minor selection decisions," *International Journal of Human Resource Management,* 17:7 July, 2006: 1254-1266.
2. Guthridge, Matthew., Asmus Komm, and Emily Lawson. "Making Talent a Strategic Priority," *McKinsey Quarterly*, no. 1 2008: 49-59.

Chapter 1

1. Gross, Jeffrey H. *Workforce Planning: 90 Day Action Plan*, Webcast, HR.com, February 7, 2007.
2. See Jeffrey H. Gross, (2008), *Workforce Planning Benchmark Study*.

Chapter 2

1. Poulos, Stacy., and Demetra Smith Nightingale. "Employment and Training Policy Implications of the Aging Baby Boom Generation," *Urban Institute,* U.S. Department of Labor, 1997.
2. *Managing the Mature Workforce*, 2005, Research Report R-1369-05-RR, [The] Conference Board.
3. Rothwell, William. *Beyond Training*. San Francisco, CA: Jossey-Bass, 1996.
4. Peters, Thomas., and Robert Waterman. 1982. *In Search of Excellence, Lessons from America's Best-Run Companies,* New York, NY: Harper & Row.
5. See William Rothwell, (1996).

6. "Workforce Planning Guidelines," *Department of Personnel,* State of Washington. 2000.
7. See Matthew Guthridge, (2008).
8. See Jeffrey H. Gross, (2008), *Workforce Planning Benchmark Study.*
9. Ibid.

Chapter 3
1. See Mary Young, (2006).
2. See Workforce Planning Guidelines, (2000).
3. Bryan, Lowell., and Claudia Joyce. *Mobilizing Minds, Creating Wealth from Talent in the 21st-Century Organization.* New York: McGraw-Hill, 2007.
4. Ibid.

Chapter 4
1. See Lowell Bryan, (2007).
2. See Jeffrey H. Gross, (2008), *Workforce Planning Benchmark Study.*
3. Ibid.
4. Ibid.
5. See Mary Young, (2006).
6. See Jeffrey H. Gross, (2008), *Workforce Planning Benchmark Study.*

Chapter 5
1. See Jeffrey H. Gross, (2008), *Workforce Planning Benchmark Study.*
2. McKinsey&Company 7-s, Back page, *McKinsey Quarterly,* no. 1, 2008.
3. See Jeffrey H. Gross, (2008), *Workforce Planning Benchmark Study.*
4. See Mary Young (2006).

Chapter 6
1. See William Rothwell, (1996).
2. De Smet, Aaron., Mark Loch, and Bill Schainger. "Anatomy of a Health Corporation," *McKinsey Quarterly* Web exclusive May, 2007.
3. Ibid.

4. See Jeffrey H. Gross, (2008), *Workforce Planning Benchmark Study.*
5. See Wilfred Geerlings, (2006).
6. Lucia, Anntoinette., and Richard Lepsinger. *The Art and Science of Competency Models.* San Francisco: Jossey-Bass, 1999.
7. Rothwell, William. *Effective Succession Planning.* San Francisco: Jossey-Bass, 2001.
8. Charan, Ram., Stephen Drotter, and James Noel. *The Leadership Pipeline, How to Build The Leadership Powered Company.* San Francisco: Jossey-Bass, 2001.

Chapter 7

1. Shippmann, Jeffrey., et al. "The Practice of Competency Modeling," *Personnel Psychology,* 53, 703-730, 2000.
2. Ibid.
3. See Jeffrey H. Gross, (2008) *Workforce Planning Benchmark Study.*
4. See Mary Young, (2006).
5. See Anntoinette Lucia, (1999).

Chapter 8

1. "Men in Black." Amblin Entertainment, MacDonald Parks Productions, 1997.
2. See Lowell Bryan, (2007).
3. Ibid.
4. See Jeffrey H. Gross, (2008), *Workforce Planning Benchmark Study.*
5. Ibid.
6. Gross, Jeffrey H. *Identifying, Attracting, and Selecting High-Performers: Differentiating Recruiter Competencies.* TopGrade Workforce Planning, Hudson, Ohio, 2007.

Chapter 9

1. McKinsey&Company 7-s, Back page, *McKinsey Quarterly,* no. 1, 2008.
2. See Jeffrey H. Gross, (2008), *Workforce Planning Benchmark Study.*
3. Gomez-Mejia, Luis., David Balkin, and Robert Cardy. *Managing Human Resources.* Englewood Cliffs, NJ: Prentice Hall, 1995.
4. Ibid.

Chapter 10

1. "What about Bob?." Touchstone Productions, 1991.

Chapter 14

1. See Jeffrey H. Gross, (2008), *Workforce Planning Benchmark Study*.
2. Ibid.
3. Mcgirt, Ellen. "Revolution in San Jose," *Fast Company, December* 2008: *134-135*.
4. See Stacy Poulos, (1997).
5. See Jeffrey H. Gross, (2007), Webcast.

Bibliography

Bryan, Lowell., and Claudia Joyce. *Mobilizing Minds, Creating Wealth from Talent in the 21st-Century Organization.* New York: McGraw-Hill, 2007.

Charan, Ram., Stephen Drotter, and James Noel. *The Leadership Pipeline, How to Build The Leadership Powered Company.* San Francisco: Jossey-Bass, 2001.

De Smet, Aaron., Mark Loch, and Bill Schainger. "Anatomy of a Health Corporation," *McKinsey Quarterly* Web exclusive May, 2007.

Geerlings, Wilfred., and Kees van Veen. "The future qualities of workforces: a simulation study of the long-term consequences of minor selection decisions," *International Journal of Human Resource Management,* 17:7 July, 2006: 1254-1266.

Gomez-Mejia, Luis., David Balkin, and Robert Cardy. *Managing Human Resources.* Englewood Cliffs, NJ: Prentice Hall, 1995.

Gross, Jeffrey H. *Workforce Planning: 90 Day Action Plan,* Webcast, HR.com, February 7, 2007.

Gross, Jeffrey H. *Identifying, Attracting, and Selecting High-Performers: Differentiating Recruiter Competencies.* TopGrade Workforce Planning, Hudson, Ohio, 2007.

Gross, Jeffrey H. *Workforce Planning Benchmark Study,* TopGrade Workforce Planning, Hudson, Ohio, 2008.

Guthridge, Matthew., Asmus Komm, and Emily Lawson. "Making Talent a Strategic Priority," *McKinsey Quarterly,* no. 1, 2008: 49-59.

"Human Capital, Key Principles for Effective Strategic Workforce Planning," *United States General Accounting Office,* Report to Congress, 2003.

Lucia, Anntoinette., and Richard Lepsinger. *The Art and Science of Competency Models*. San Francisco: Jossey-Bass, 1999.

Managing the Mature Workforce, Research Report R-1369-05-RR, [The] Conference Board, 2005.

Mcgirt, Ellen. "Revolution in San Jose," *Fast Company, December* 2008: *134-135.*

McKinsey&Company 7-s, Back page, *McKinsey Quarterly*, no. 1, 2008.

"Men in Black." Amblin Entertainment, MacDonald Parks Productions, 1997.

Peters, Thomas., and Robert Waterman. 1982. *In Search of Excellence, Lessons from America's Best-Run Companies,* New York, NY: Harper & Row.

Poulos, Stacy., and Demetra Smith Nightingale. "Employment and Training Policy Implications of the Aging Baby Boom Generation," *Urban Institute,* U.S. Department of Labor, 1997.

Rothwell, William. *Beyond Training*. San Francisco, CA: Jossey-Bass, 1996.

Rothwell, William. *Effective Succession Planning.* San Francisco: Jossey-Bass, 2001.

Shippmann, Jeffrey., et al. "The Practice of Competency Modeling," *Personnel Psychology,* 53, 703-730, 2000.

Young, Mary. *Strategic Workforce Planning,* Working Group Research Report, [The] Conference Board, 2006.

"What about Bob?." Touchstone Productions, 1991.

"Workforce Planning Guidelines," *Department of Personnel,* State of Washington, 2000.

Index

R
Recruiters
143, 146, 149, 150, 153

Replacement Policy
v, 95, 117-119, 126, 185, 188, 201

ROI (Return on Investment)
31, 48, 216

S
Strategic Segmentation
iv, v, 85, 86, 90, 91, 123, 124

T
Talent Acquisition
v, 3, 16, 50, 55, 128, 137, 142-154, 168, 183, 184, 188

Taskforce
iv, v, vi, 8, 10, 12, 34, 43-46, 50, 57-65, 72, 73, 84, 86, 89-91, 94, 108, 111, 124, 125

ABOUT THE AUTHOR

In the last twenty years, Jeff Gross has brought ground breaking programs of change and improvement to many public and private organizations. He is a thought leader in workforce planning, frequent lecturer, speaker and author.

Authored books include:

Workforce Planning: 90 Day Action Plan™ Participant Guide

Workforce Planning: 90 Day Action Plan™ Field Manual

Workforce Planning: 90 Day Action Plan ™ Handbook

Workforce Planning 2020

www.workforceplanning2020.com